Old-Time Hymns & Gospel Favorites
for Mountain Dulcimer

arranged by
Anne Lough

© 2010 BY MEL BAY PUBLICATIONS, INC. ALL RIGHTS RESERVED.
WWW.MELBAY.COM

Table of Contents

Introduction 3
Left-Hand Technique 4
Additional Markings..4
Ionian Mode - Tunes in DAA 5
Amazing Grace 6
Farther Along 8
The Haven of Rest 10
Heavenly Sunlight 12
I'll Fly Away 14
Keep on the Sunny Side..16
Leaning on the Everlasting Arms 18
Life's Railway to Heaven 20
Nearer My God To Thee..22
Pass Me Not, O Gentle Savior 24
Precious Memories...26
Softly and Tenderly 28
Sweet By and By 30
Twilight is Falling 32
Unclouded Day 34
What a Friend We Have in Jesus 36
When the Roll is Called Up Yonder 38
Mixolydian Mode - Tunes in DAD..41
Blessed Assurance 42
Come Thou Fount (Nettleton) 44
Come Thou Fount (Warrenton) 46
Fairest Lord Jesus 48
He Leadeth Me...50
Holy, Holy, Holy 52
It is Well With My Soul 54
Just a Rose Will Do 56
Just As I Am 58
Sweet Hour of Prayer 60
Sweet Hour of Prayer, Finger-Picked 62
There is a Fountain 64
Trust and Obey...66
Were You There 68
When the Morning Comes 70
When They Ring Those Golden Bells 72
Where We'll Never Grow Old 74
Whispering Hope..76
Reverse Ionian - Tunes in DGD..79
Dwelling in Beulah Land 80
For the Beauty of the Earth 82
I Love to Tell the Story 84
In the Garden 86
Rock of Ages 88
Victory in Jesus 90
About the Author 92

Introduction

"What a fellowship, what a joy divine!"

The words to this old hymn express the spirit of congregational singing, as well as the spirit I have felt among dulcimer players as we share music together. So many times it is the old hymns that bring folks together, making melody on instruments, with voices and with the heart. The enduring quality and message of these hymns seem to transcend time, place, denomination or creed.

Over the years, I have enjoyed playing and singing these hymns in settings ranging from the privacy of my living room to audiences of several thousand. They seem to weave their spell no matter the make up or size of the audience. I pray that as you play and share the tunes in this collection you, as well, will be filled with the spirit of these hymns.

The songs in the book are arranged in sections according to the tuning used. Many of the old hymns work well in the traditional Ionian, or DAA tuning, because of their melodic range. Another section includes arrangements in Mixolydian, or DAD tuning, and the final section has arrangements in DGD, making them more accessible for most voice ranges. An explanation of the tuning will be found at the beginning of each section.

Players of all levels will be able to enjoy these tunes. There are some very simple arrangements with mostly melody and drone, while others are much more complicated. It is important to keep in mind that much of the beauty and appeal of the songs, as well as of the dulcimer, is in their simplicity. For the less experienced player, try playing the more challenging tunes with just the melody and open drone strings. This will still sound nice and the chord accompaniments can be added later, after more practice and work with chord shapes.

Enjoy!

Left-Hand Technique

Hammer-ons, pull-offs and slides are left-hand finger techniques commonly used by guitar players. They are very effective on the dulcimer as well. Becoming efficient in the use of these can add a new dimension and flowing quality to your melodies

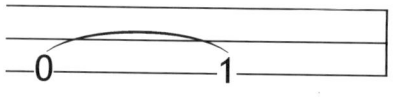

A slurred line on top connecting two notes indicates a hammer-on. The first note is strummed, then the second note is sounded by "hammering" down with another finger.

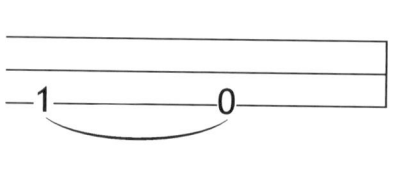

A slurred line on the bottom connecting two notes indicates a pull-off. The first note is held down and strummed, then the second note sounded by pushing down and pulling off (a plucking motion) with the same finger to a lower note. If pulling off to a lower fret other than 0, it must already be held down with another finger.

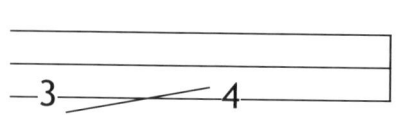

A straight line connecting two notes indicates a slide. The first note is strummed, then the second note sounded by sliding the same finger to the correct fret while pressing down slightly against the fretboard.

With these techniques, two notes are sounded for one strum, the second note being achieved by the action of the left hand. These are also very effective in more up-tempo tunes, allowing for cleaner, faster execution of the notes.

Additional Markings

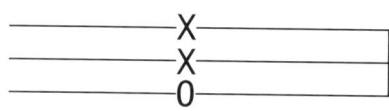

An X on a tab line indicates the string or strings should not be sounded. The string with the fret number would be picked or plucked by itself.

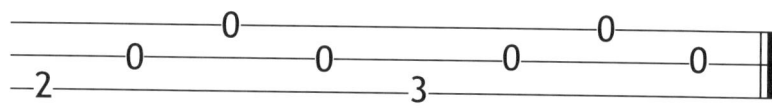

When the numbers on the tab lines are offset, it indicates a finger picking pattern.

If there are no 0's on a tab line, assume it is strummed open.

Right-hand technique is also very important. Picking individual strings at times with your pick instead using of a full strum can add interest and musicality to your playing. This will be indicated in some of the arrangements in the above manner.

Occasionally there will be a suggestion of fingering, to aid in a smooth transition from one chord to the next. TH = thumb, I = index finger, M = middle finger, R = ring finger and P = pinky.

A general note about fingering:
It is well worth the time in any arrangement to experiment with different fingering to see what works best for your fingers. What works best for one person may not be as comfortable or efficient for another. The goal is to move from one position to another without breaking the sound, avoiding any unnecessary re-configuration of the fingers. If the fingers stay curved over the fretboard, as if you were playing the piano, you will find that many times there is a finger already in place, ready to hold down the fret.

The Ionian Mode or DAA

The songs in the first section are in the Ionian mode. This mode was the original "major" tuning and the most frequently used on the mountain dulcimer before the addition of the 6 1/2 fret. It is many times referred to as **DAA**, **Do-Sol-Sol**, or **1-5-5** tuning, as it is based on the relationship between the first and fifth scale step, or the **Do** and **Sol** of a scale. Ionian is a wonderful tuning for many of the old time folk songs, hymns, and any song whose melody uses a lot of notes below the **Do**, or root note of the scale. All, or most of the notes of the melody, can then be played on the melody string. This gives a fuller, more "dulcimeristic" sound and allows for fuller chord arrangements, with all three strings being sounded.

To tune to this mode, tune the bass string to **D** below middle C. Next tune the middle string and both melody strings to the **A** below middle C. The dulcimer can also be tuned to itself once the pitch of the bass string is established. The pitch for the middle and melody strings can be sounded by plucking the bass string while holding it down on the fourth fret. This sounds the **Sol** or fifth note of the scale.

You are now tuned in **D Ionian (DAA)**. The starting point, or **Do**, of the scale on the melody string is the third fret. Play this scale up and down a few times, starting on the third fret and going up to the tenth, skipping the 6 1/2 fret. Then play the intervals of the third, fifth, seventh and tenth frets up and down several times, outlining the notes of the D or I chord, upon which many melodies are based.

Keep in mind that this is a relative, or movable tuning system. If you want to tune your dulcimer a little lower, such as the key of C, simply tune the bass string to C and the other three to the fifth note of that scale, or G. A higher pitch, such as E would be tuned EBB. The important thing is the relationship between the **Do** and **Sol**.

Amazing Grace

Arr. by Anne Lough

Newton

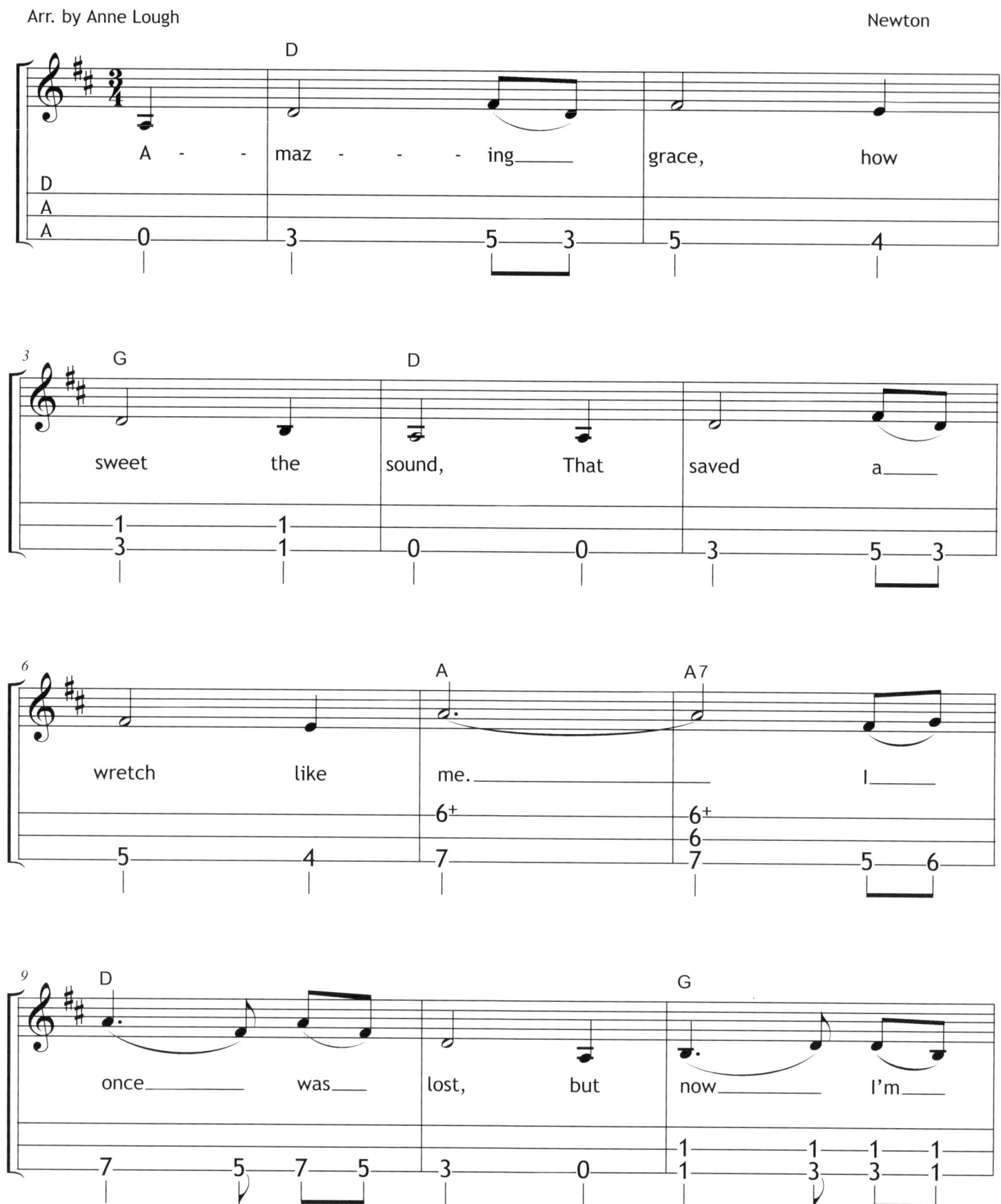

6

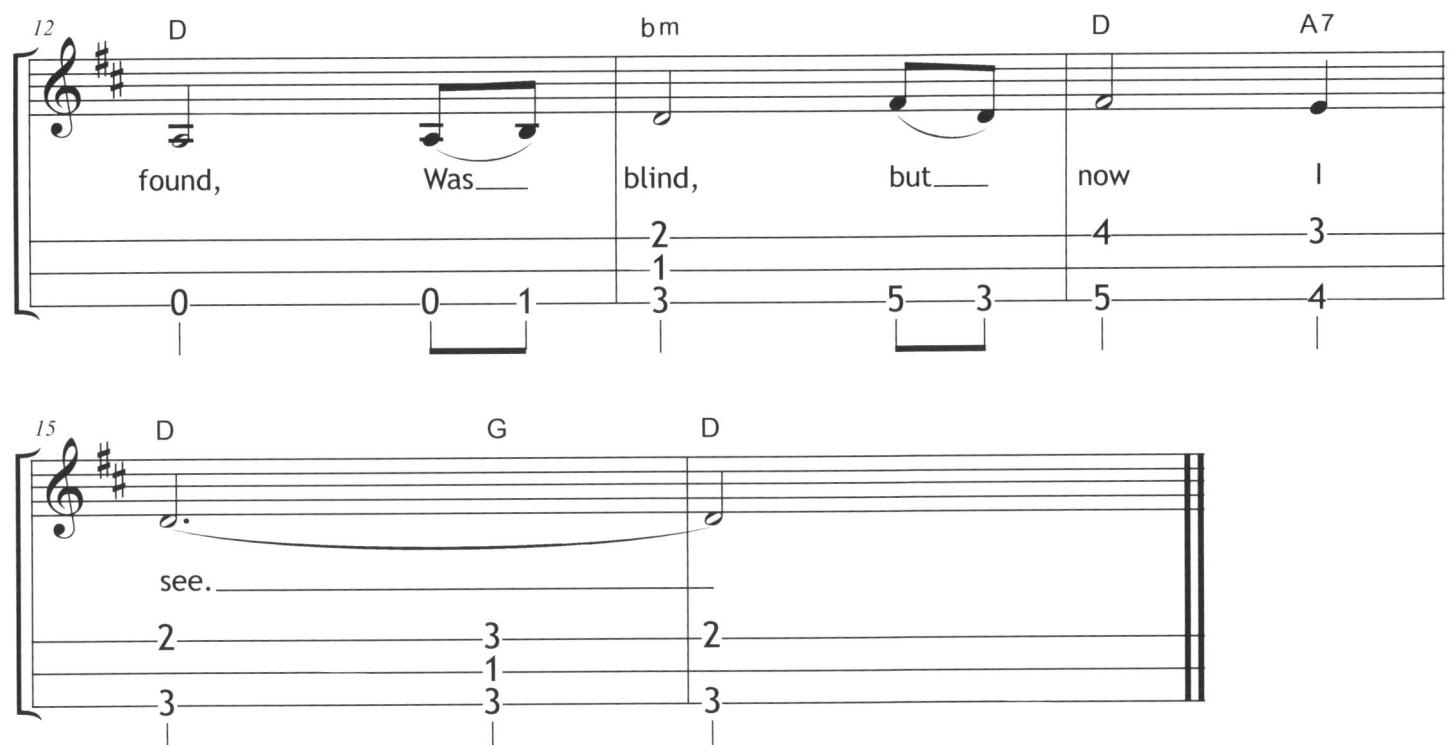

2. 'Twas grace that taught my heart to fear,
And grace my fears relieved;
How precious did that grace appear,
The hour I first believed.

3. Through many dangers, toils and snares,
I have already come;
'Tis grace that brought me safe thus far,
And grace will lead me home.

4. When we've been there ten thousand years,
Bright shining as the sun,
We've no less days to sing God's praise
Than when we first begun.

Farther Along

2. When death has come and taken our loved ones,
It leaves our home so lonely and drear,
Then do we wonder why others prosper,
Living so wicked, year after year.
                Chorus

3. Faithful till death said our loving Master,
A few more days to labor and wait;
Toils of the road will then seem as nothing,
As we sweep thru the beautiful gate.
                Chorus

4. When we see Jesus, coming in glory,
When He comes from His home in the sky;
Then we shall meet Him, in that bright mansion,
We'll understand it, all by and by.
                Chorus

The Haven of Rest

Arr. by Anne Lough

Gilmour/Moore

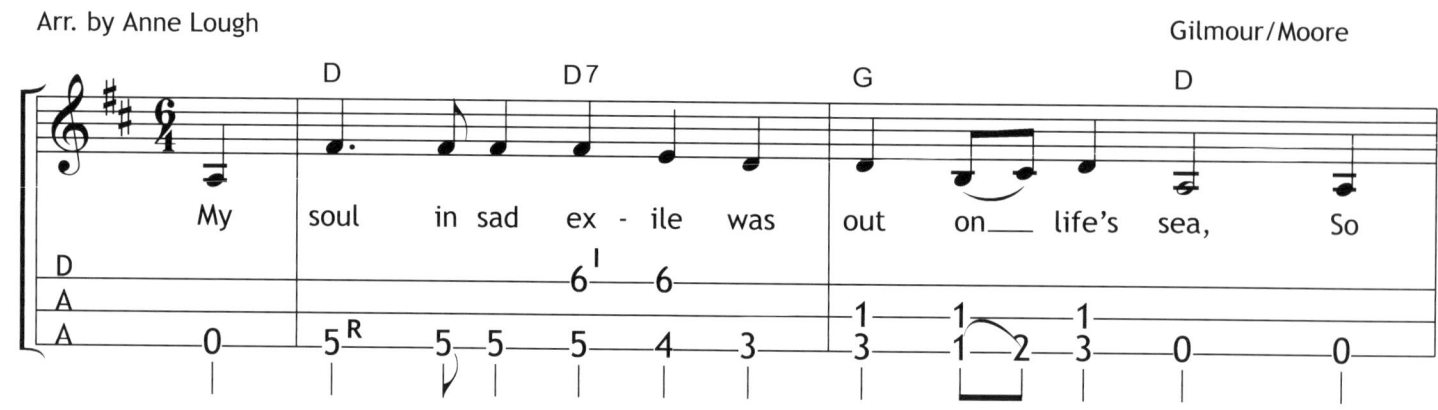
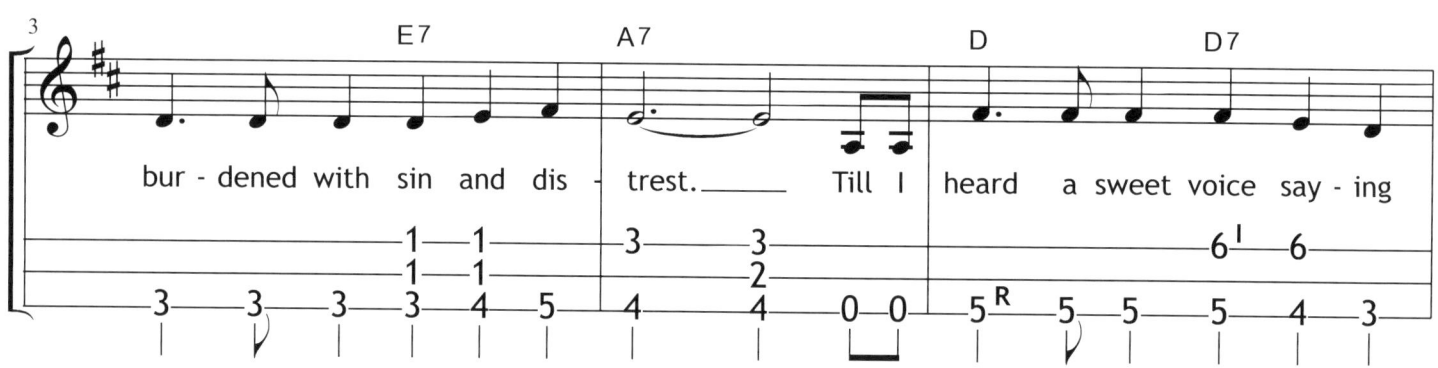

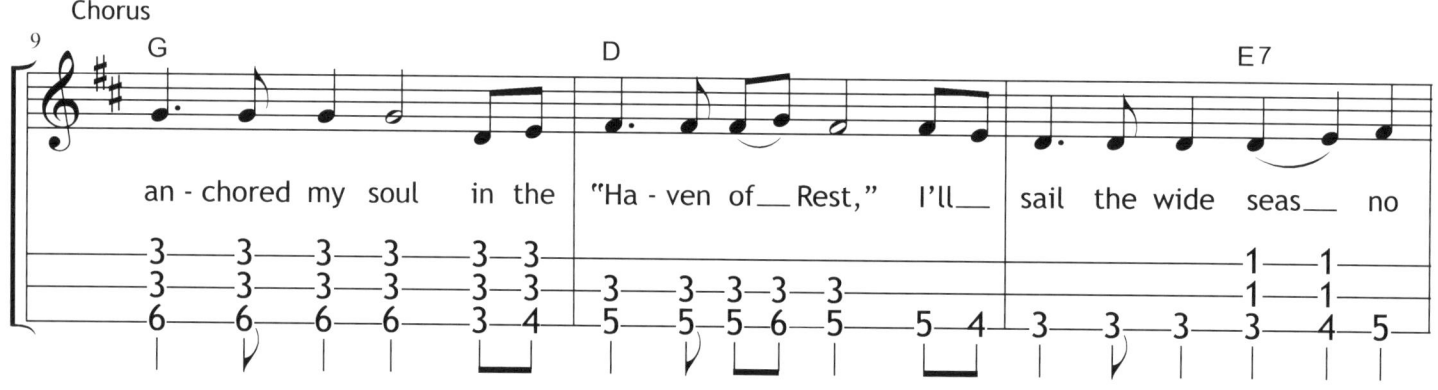

2. I yielded myself to His tender embrace, And in faith taking hold of the Word,
My fetters fell off, and I anchored my soul; The "Haven of Rest" is my Lord.
                              Chorus

3. The song of my soul since the Lord made me whole, Has been the old story so blest,
Of Jesus, who'll save whosoever will have, A home in the "Haven of Rest!"
                              Chorus

4. How precious the thought that we all may recline, Like John the beloved and blest,
On Jesus' strong arm, where no tempest can harm, Secure in the "Haven of Rest!"
                              Chorus

5. Oh, come to the Saviour, He patiently waits, To save by His power divine,
Come anchor your soul in the "Haven of Rest," and say, "My Beloved is mine."
                              Chorus

Heavenly Sunlight

Arr. by Anne Lough
Zelly/Cook

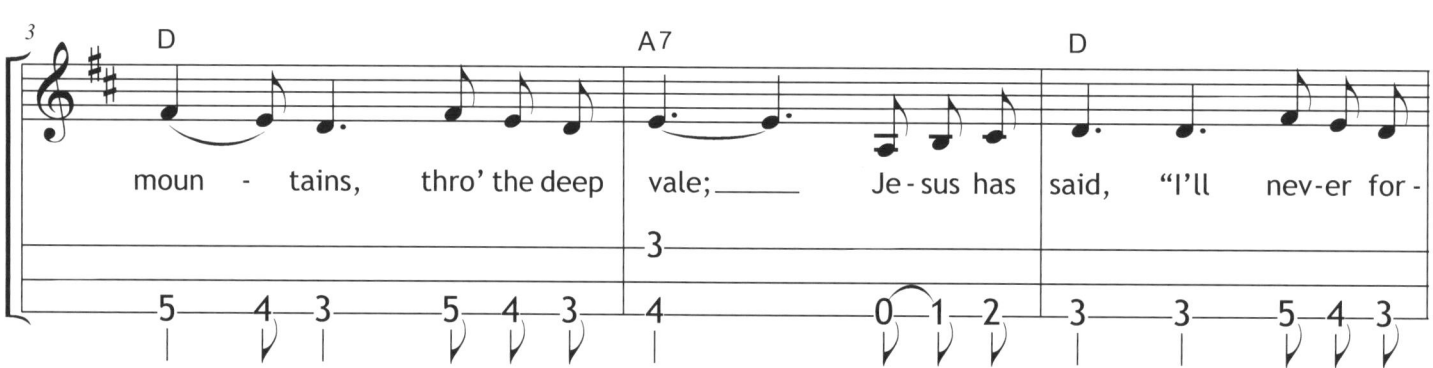
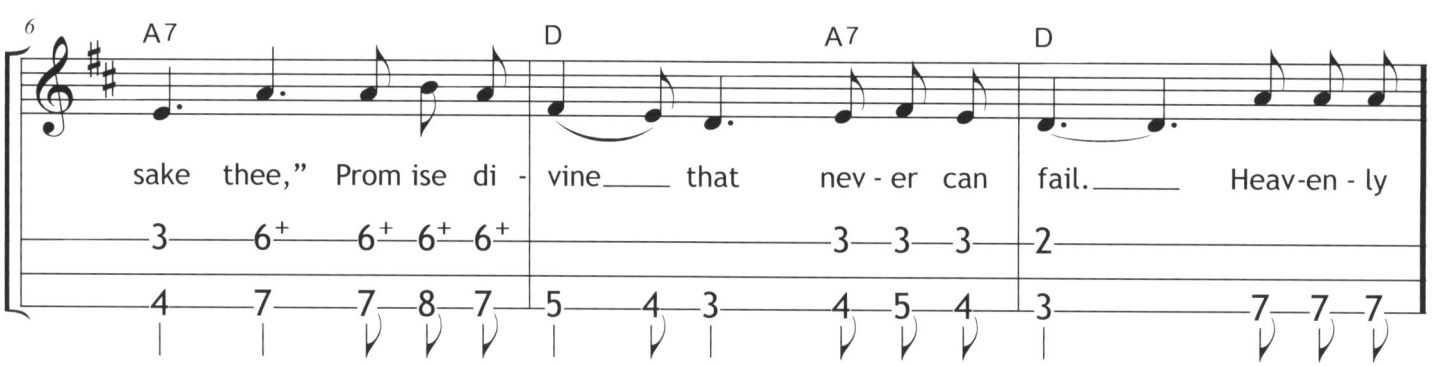
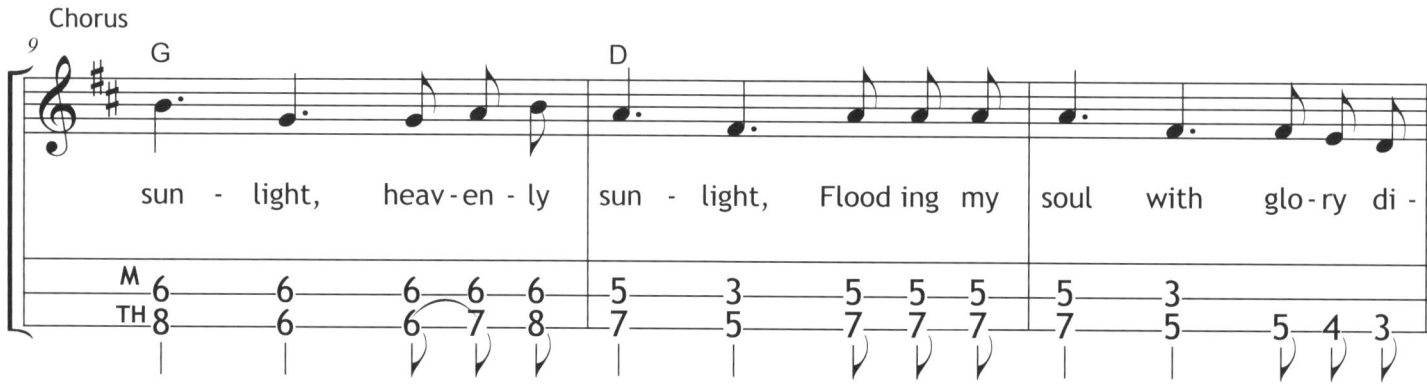

2. Shadows around me, shadows above me,
Never conceal my Savior and Guide;
He is the light, in Him is no darkness;
Ever I'm walking close to His side.
          Chorus

3. In the bright sunlight, ever rejoicing,
Pressing my way to mansions above;
Singing His praises gladly I'm walking,
Walking in sunlight, sunlight of love.
          Chorus

I'll Fly Away

Arr. by Anne Lough

Albert E. Brumley

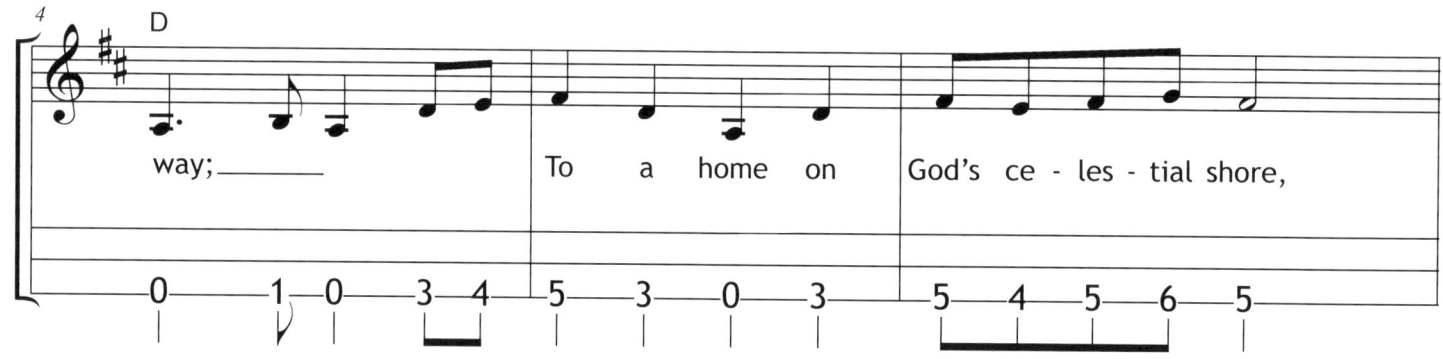
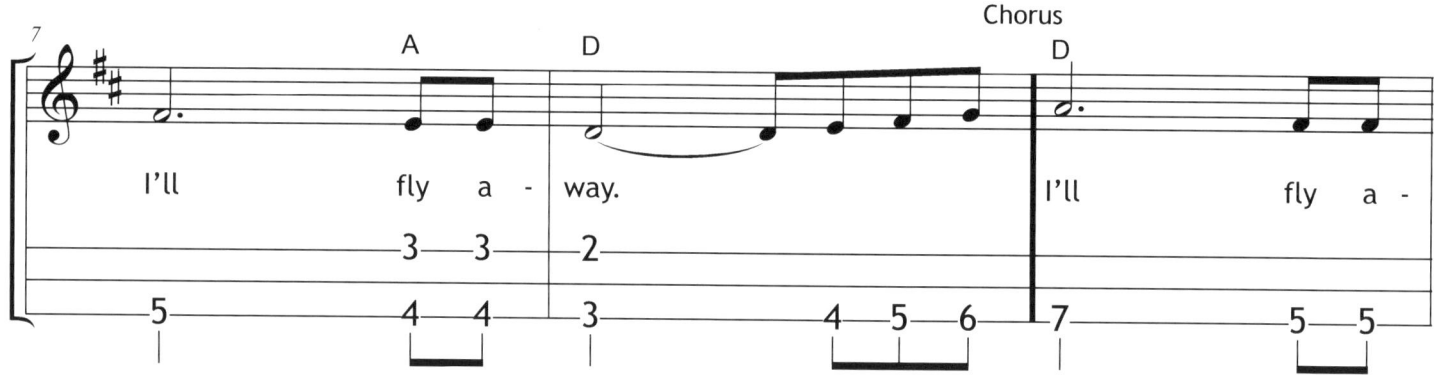
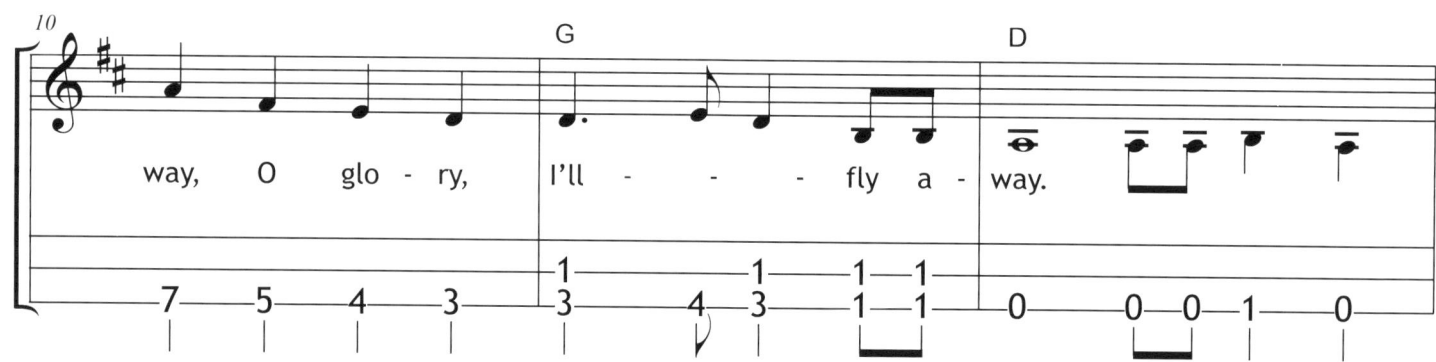

© 1932 in "Wonderful Message" by Hartford Music, Co.
Renewed © 1960 by Albert E. Brumley and Sons/SESAC. Administered by ICG. All Rights Reserved. Used by Permission.

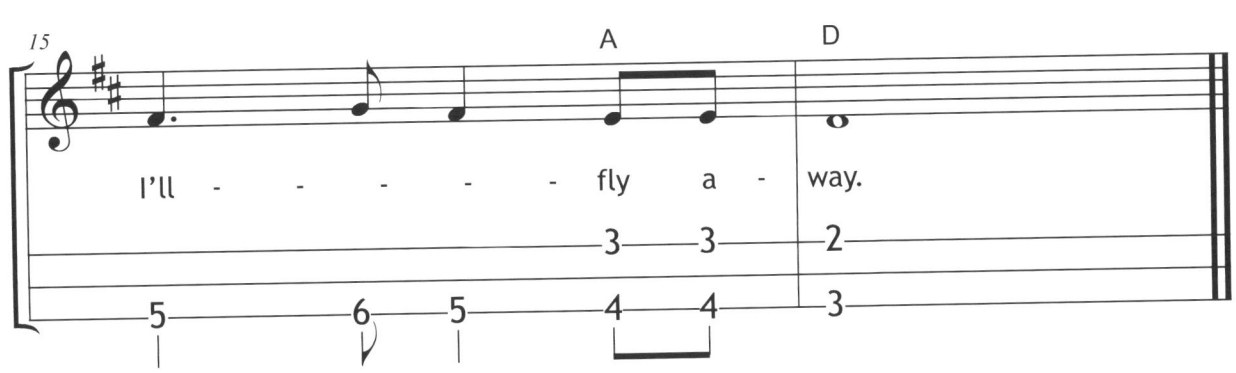

2. When the shadows of this life have grown, I'll fly away,
Like a bird from prison bars has flown, I'll fly away.
                Chorus

3. Just a few more weary days and then, I'll fly away,
To a home where joys shall never end, I'll fly away.
                Chorus

Keep on the Sunny Side of Life

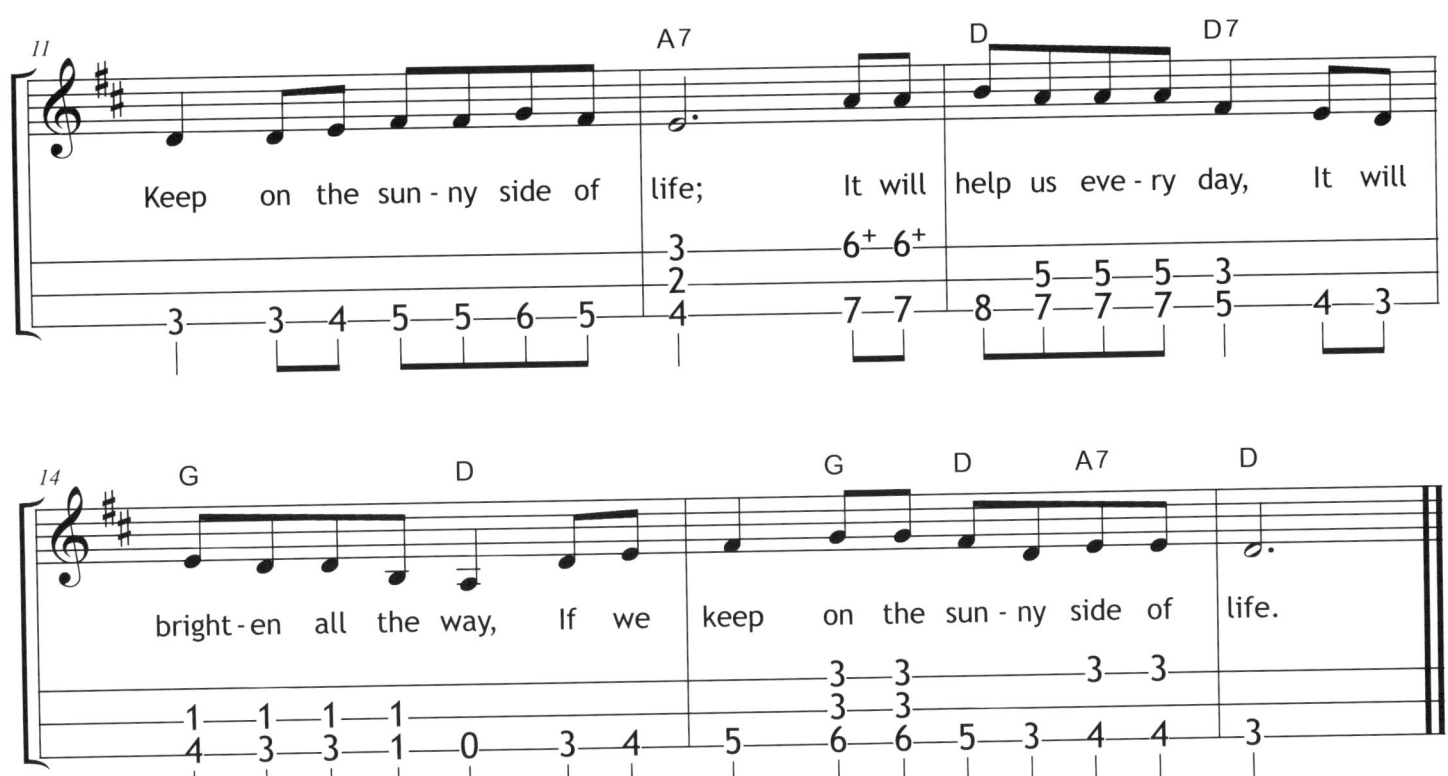

2. Tho' the storm in it's fury rage today,
Crushing hopes that we cherish so dear;
Storm and cloud will in time pass away,
The sun will shine again bright and clear.
           Chorus

3. Let us greet with a song of hope each day,
Tho' the moments be cloudy or fair;
Let us trust in our Saviour alway,
Who keepeth ev'ry one in His care.
           Chorus

Leaning on the Everlasting Arms

Arr. by Anne Lough

Hoffman/Showalter

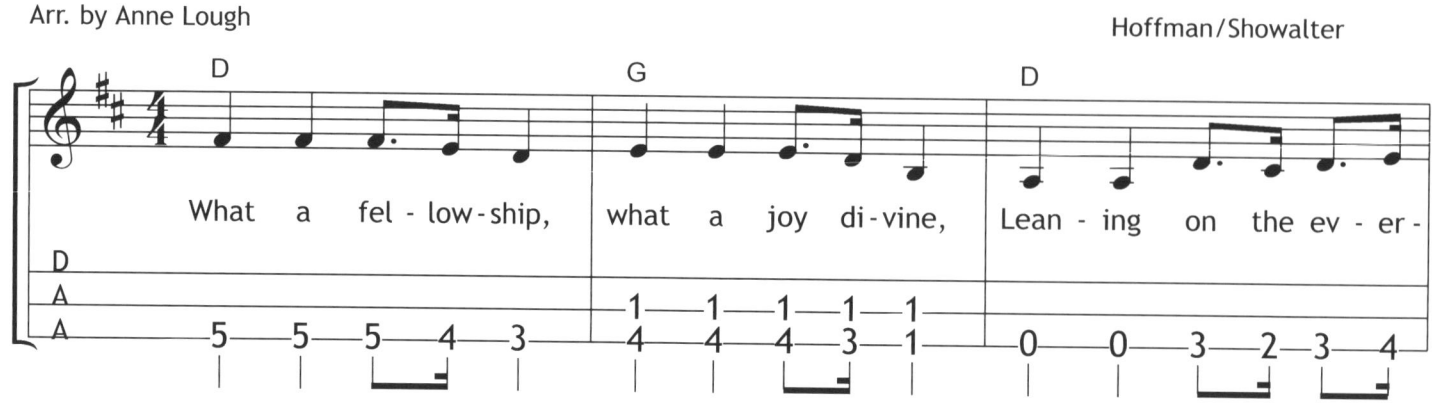

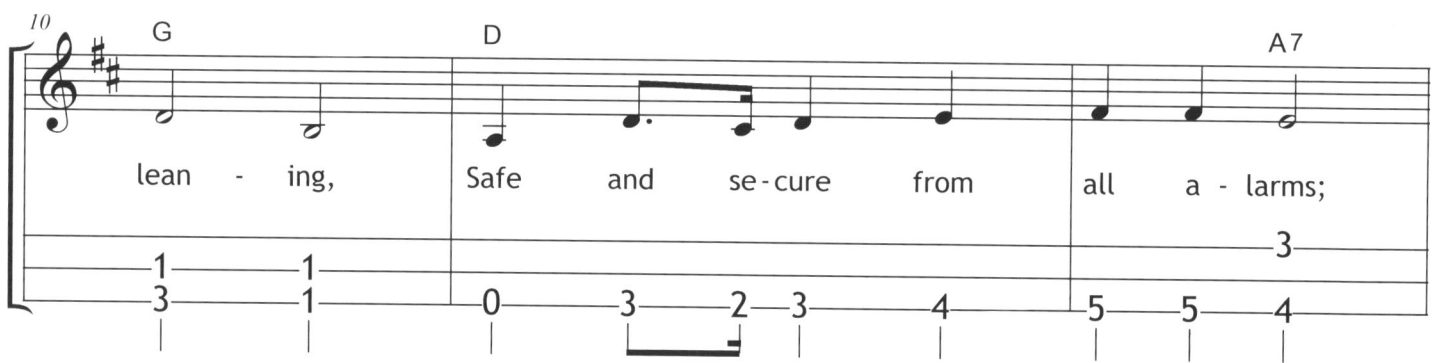

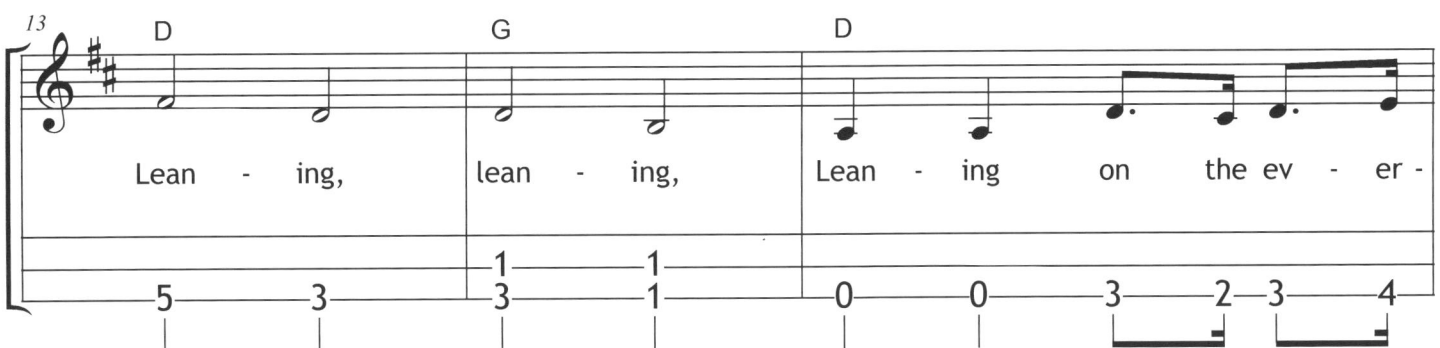

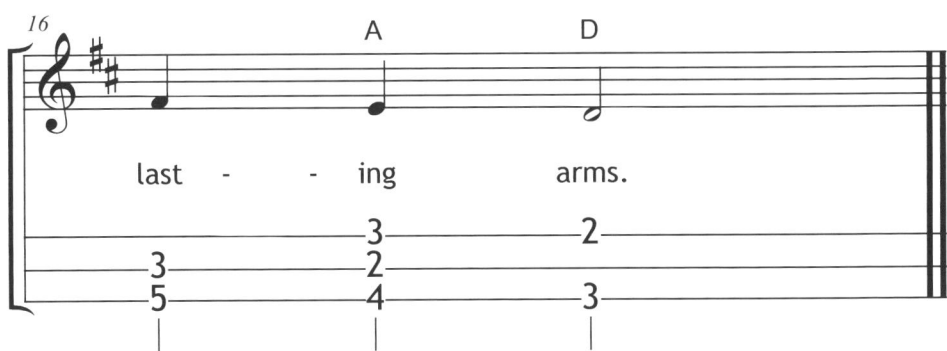

2. O how sweet to walk in the pilgrim way, Leaning on the everlasting arms;
O how bright the path grows from day to day, Leaning on the everlasting arms.
     Chorus

3. What have I do dread, what have I to fear, Leaning on the everlasting arms;
I have blessed peace with my Lord so near, Leaning on the everlasting arms.
     Chorus

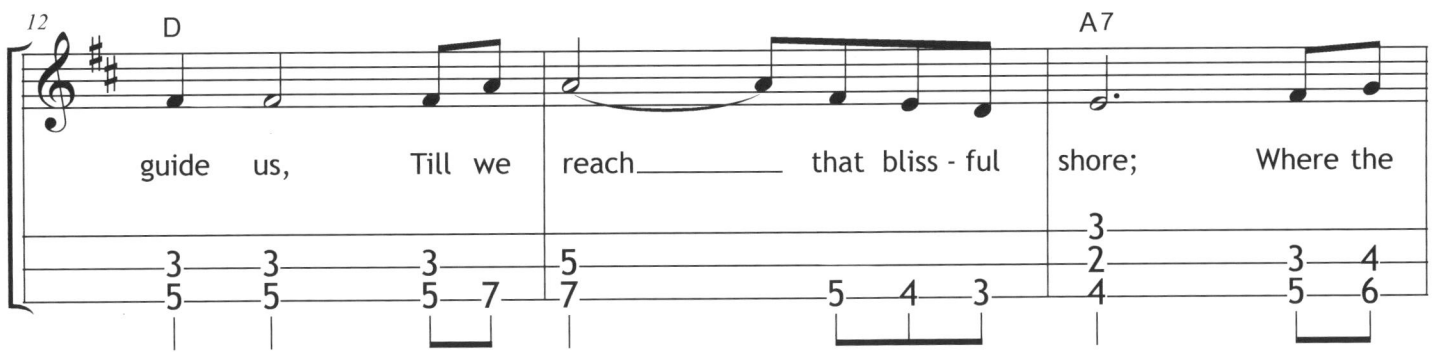

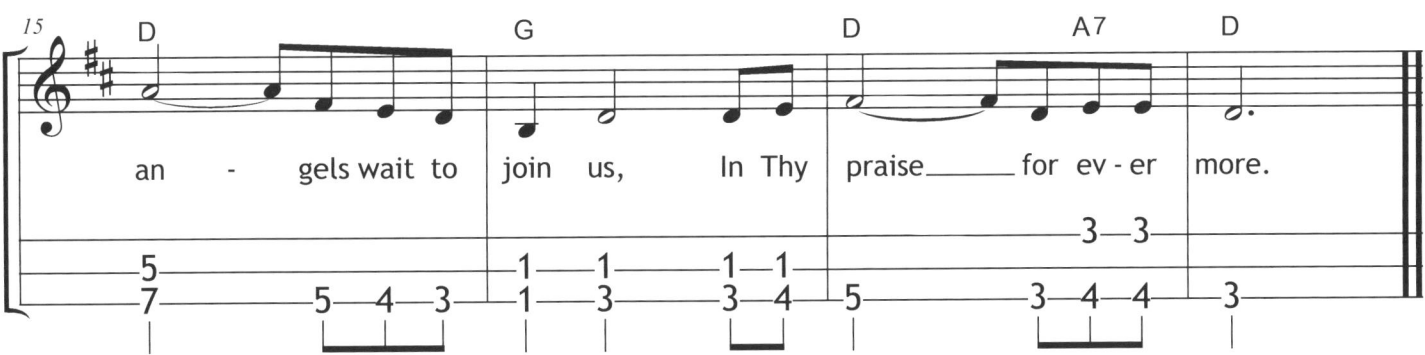

2. You will roll up grades of trial, You will cross the bridge of strife;
See that Christ is your conductor On this light'ning train of life;
Always mindful of obstruction, Do your duty, never fail;
Keep your hand upon the throttle, And your eye upon the rail.
                Chorus

3. You will often find obstructions, Look for storms of wind and rain;
On a fill, or curve, or trestle, They will almost ditch your train;
Put your trust alone in Jesus, Never falter, never fail;
Keep your hand upon the throttle, And your eye upon the rail.
                Chorus

4. As you roll across the trestle, Spanning Jordan's swelling tide;
You behold the Union Depot, Into which your train will glide;
There you'll meet the superintendent, God the Father, God the Son,
With the hearty joyous plaudit, "Weary pilgrim, welcome home!"
                Chorus

Nearer, My God, to Thee

Arr. by Anne Lough

Adams/Mason

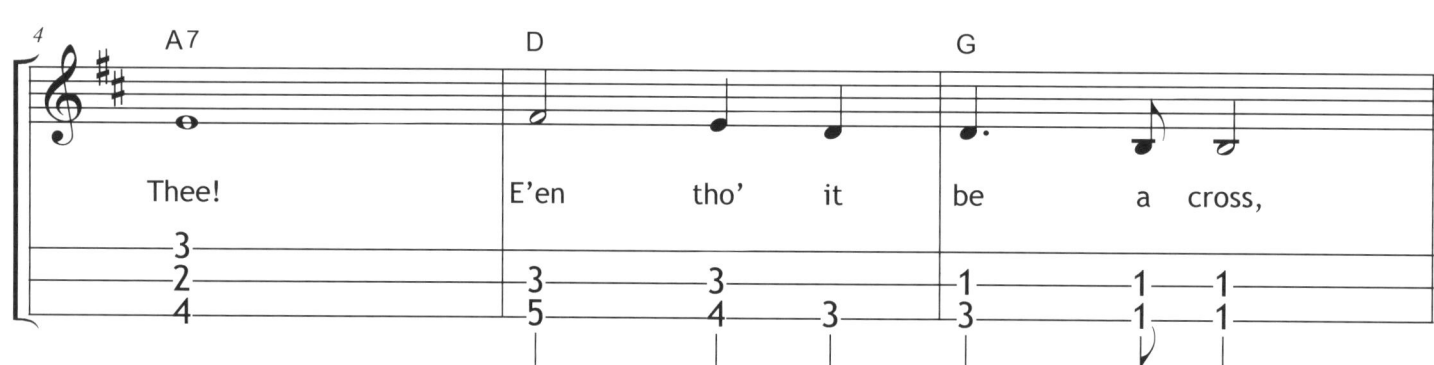
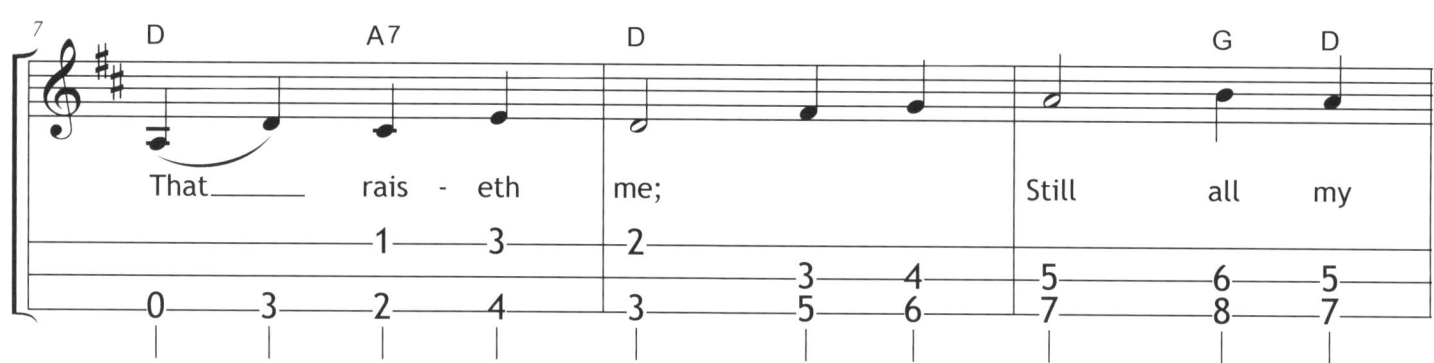
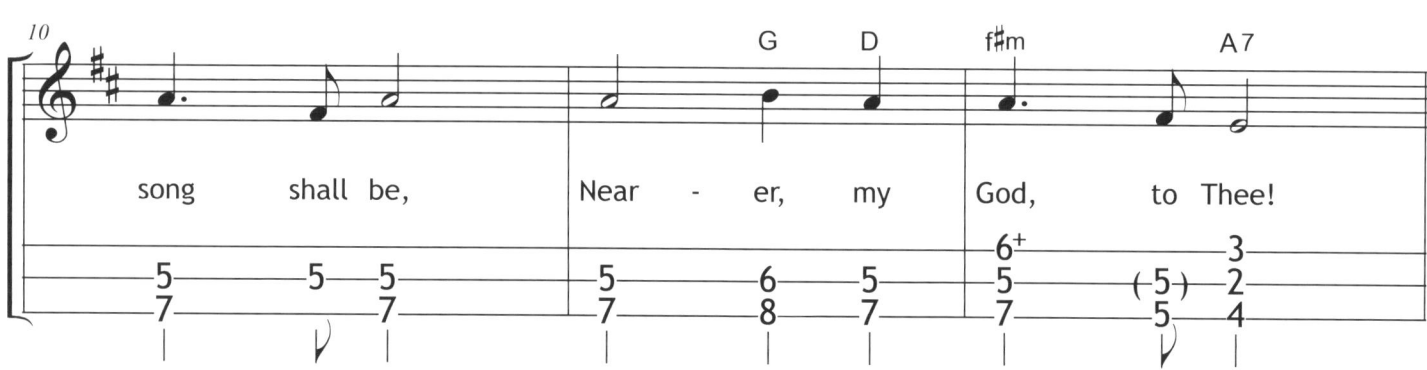

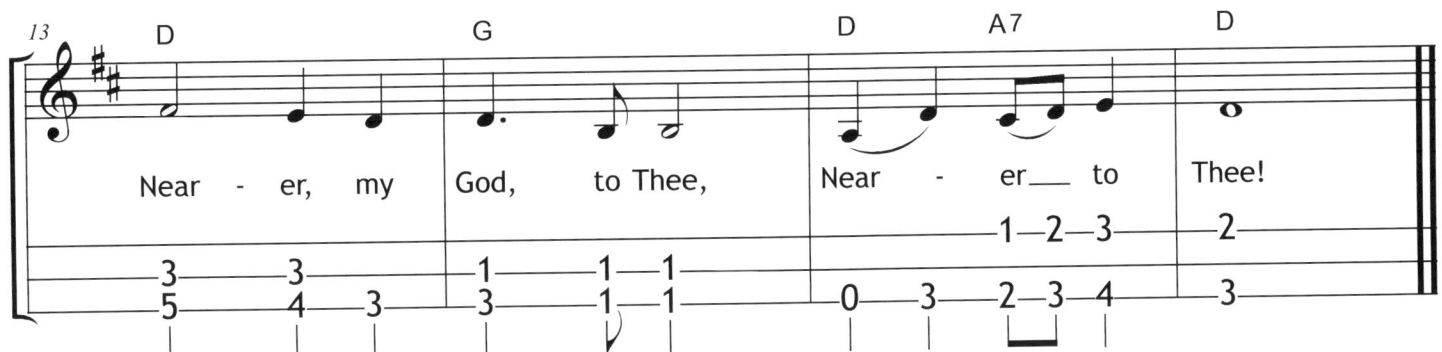

2. There let the way appear, steps unto heav'n;
All that Thou sendest me, In mercy giv'n.
Angels to beckon me Nearer, my God to Thee!
Nearer, my God, to Thee, Nearer to Thee!

3. Then with my waking tho'ts, Bright with Thy praise;
Out of my stony griefs Bethel I'll raise.
So by my woes to be Nearer, my God, to Thee!
Nearer, my God, to Thee, Nearer to Thee!

Pass Me Not, O Gentle Savior

Arr. by Anne Lough

Crosby/Doane

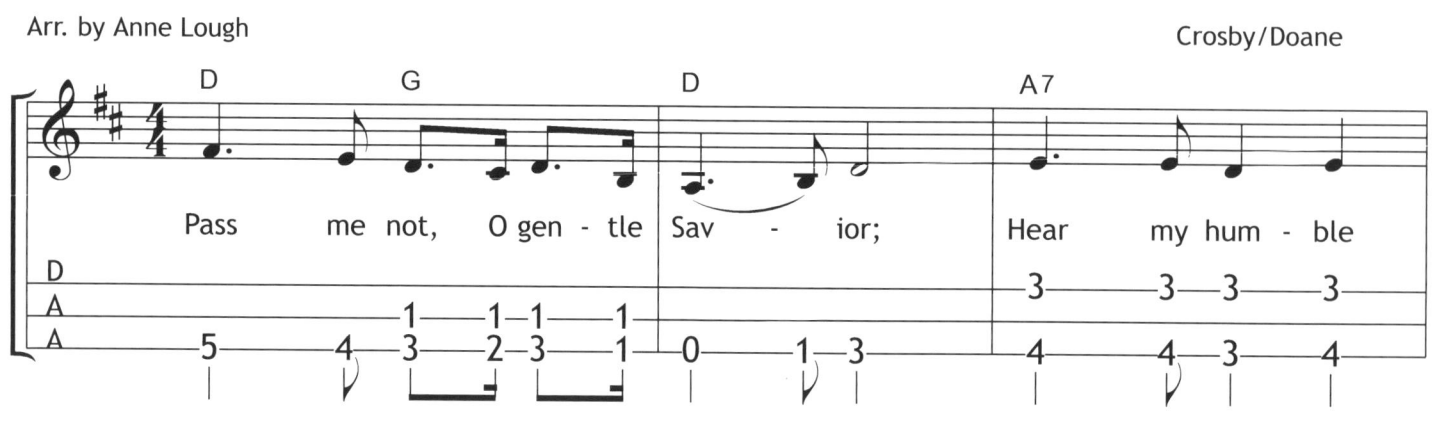

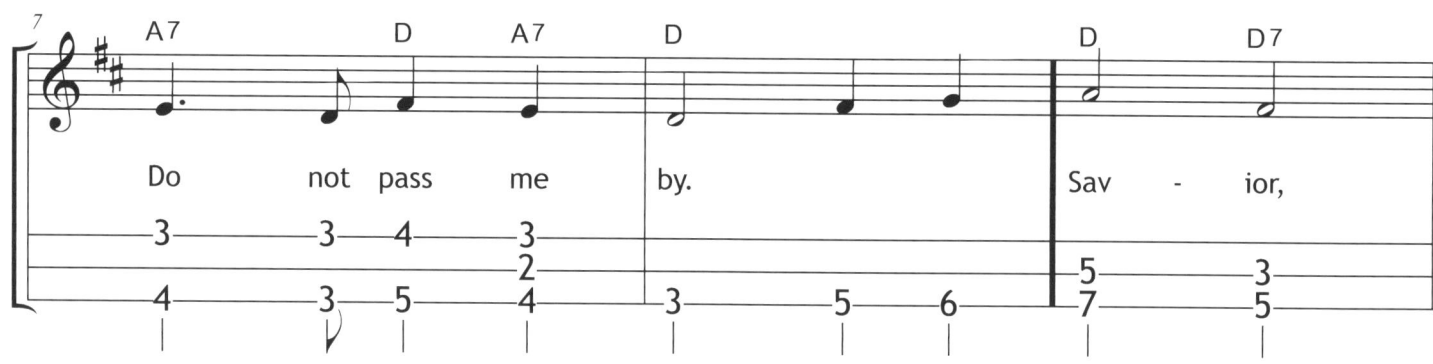
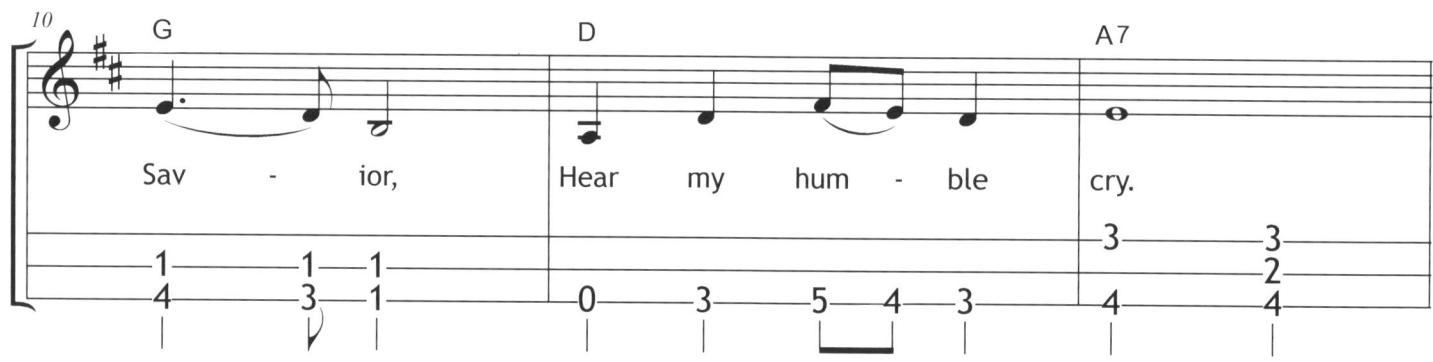

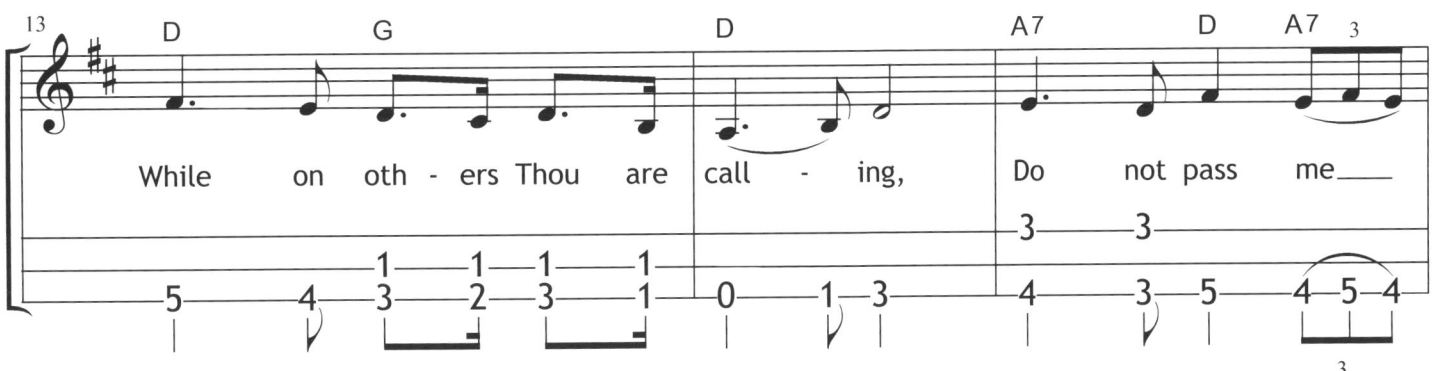

2. Let me at the throne of mercy, Find a sweet relief;
Kneeling there in deep contrition, Help my unbelief.
　　　　　　Chorus

3. Trusting only in Thy merit, Would I seek Thy face.
Heal my wounded, broken spirit; Save me by Thy grace.
　　　　　　Chorus

4. Thou, the Spring of all my comfort, More than life to me,
Whom have I on earth beside Thee? Whom in heav'n but Thee?
　　　　　　Chorus

Precious Memories

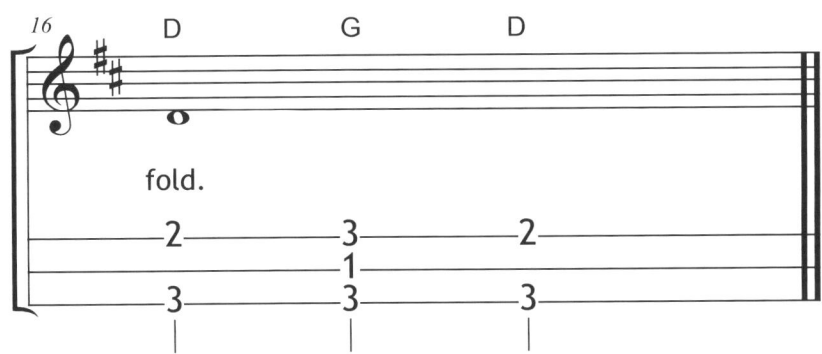

2. Precious father, loving mother,
Fly across the lonely years;
And old home scenes of my childhood
In fond memory appear.
        Chorus

3. As I travel on life's pathway,
Know not what the years may hold;
As I ponder, hope grows fonder,
Precious mem'ries flood my soul.
        Chorus

Softly and Tenderly

Arr. by Anne Lough

Will L. Thompson

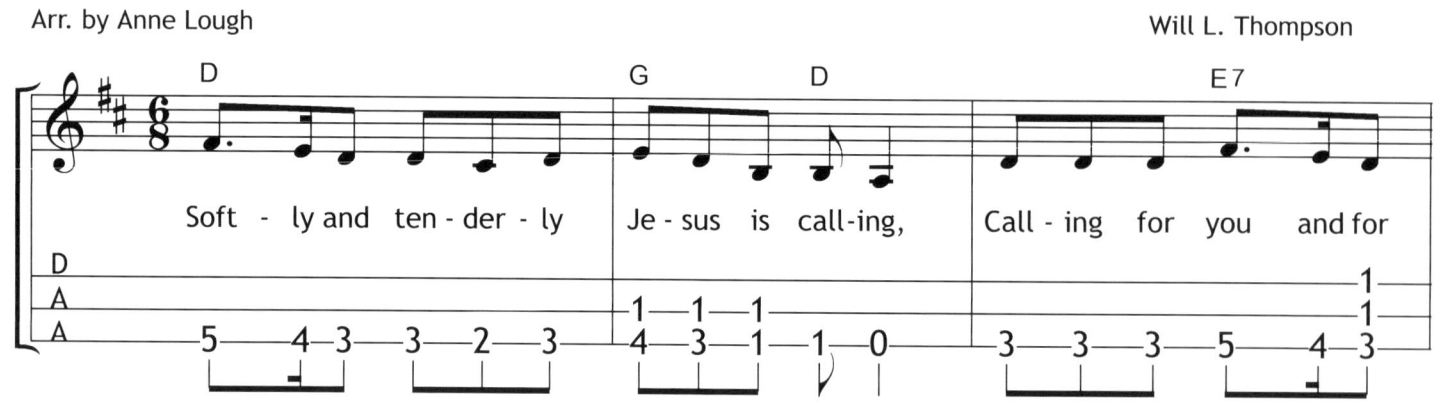

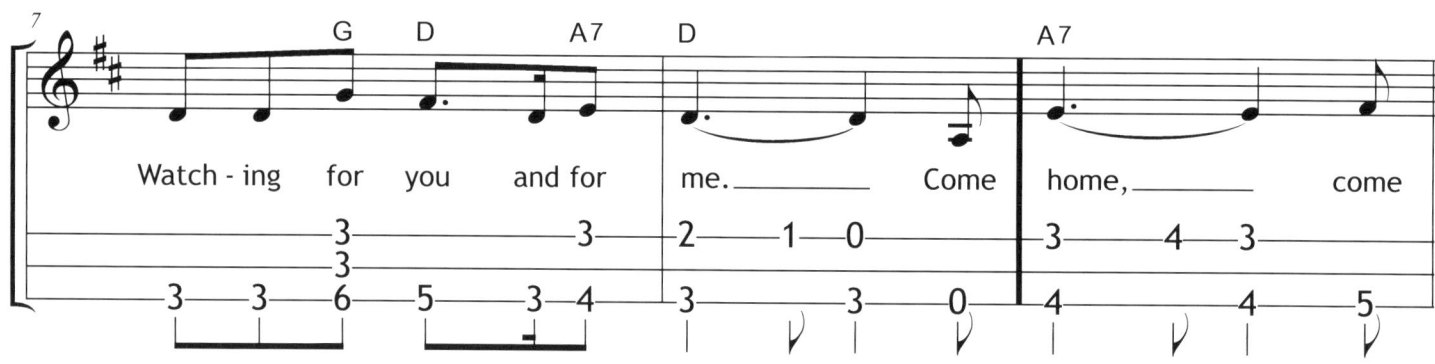

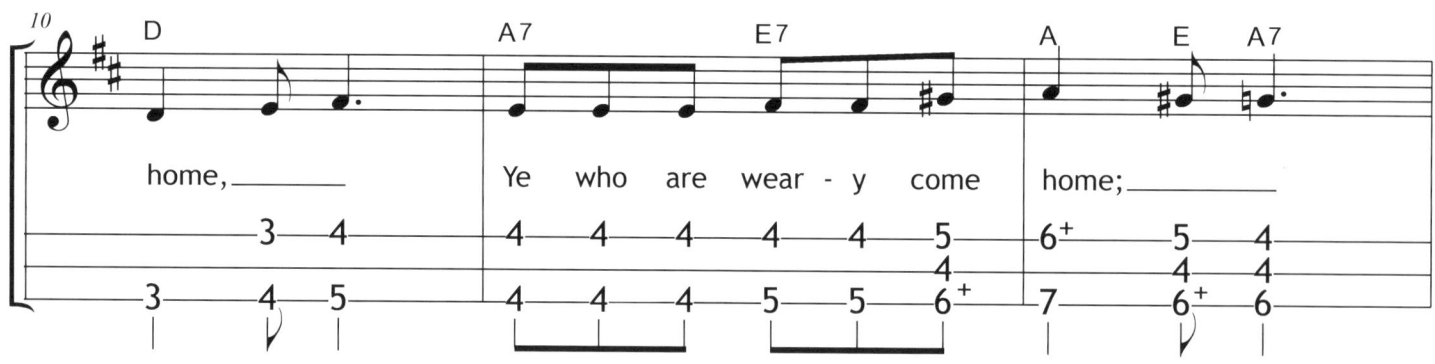

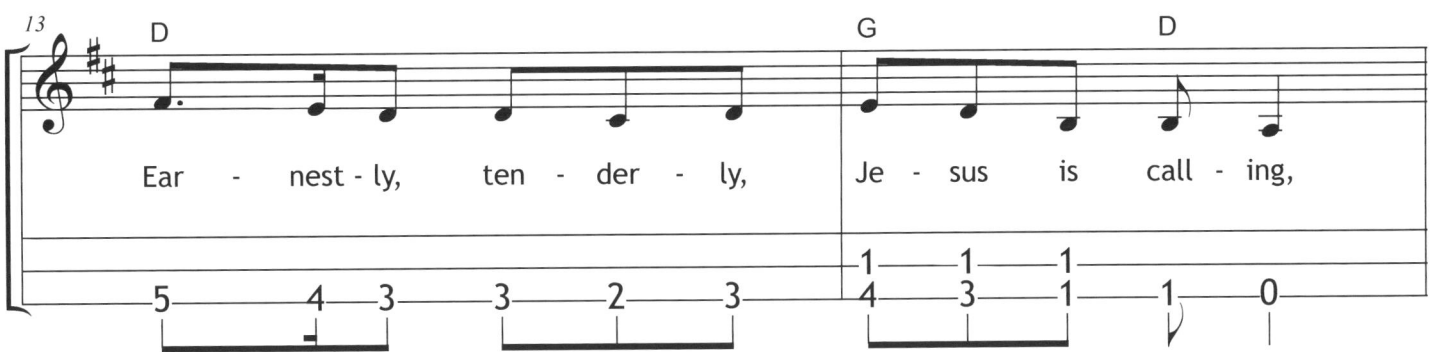

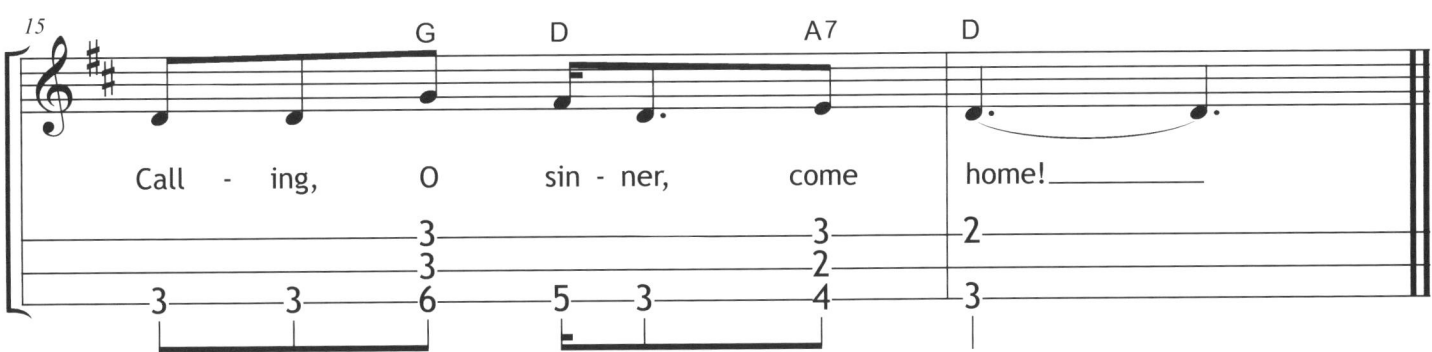

2. Why should we tarry when Jesus is pleading,
Pleading for you and for me?
Why should we linger and heed not His mercies,
Mercies for you and for me?
     Chorus

3. Time is now fleeting, the moments are passing,
Passing from you and from me;
Shadows are gathering, deathbeds are coming,
Coming for you and for me.
     Chorus

4. Oh! for the wonderful love He has promised,
Promised for you and for me;
Tho' we have sinned He has mercy and pardon,
Pardon for you and for me.
     Chorus

Sweet By and By

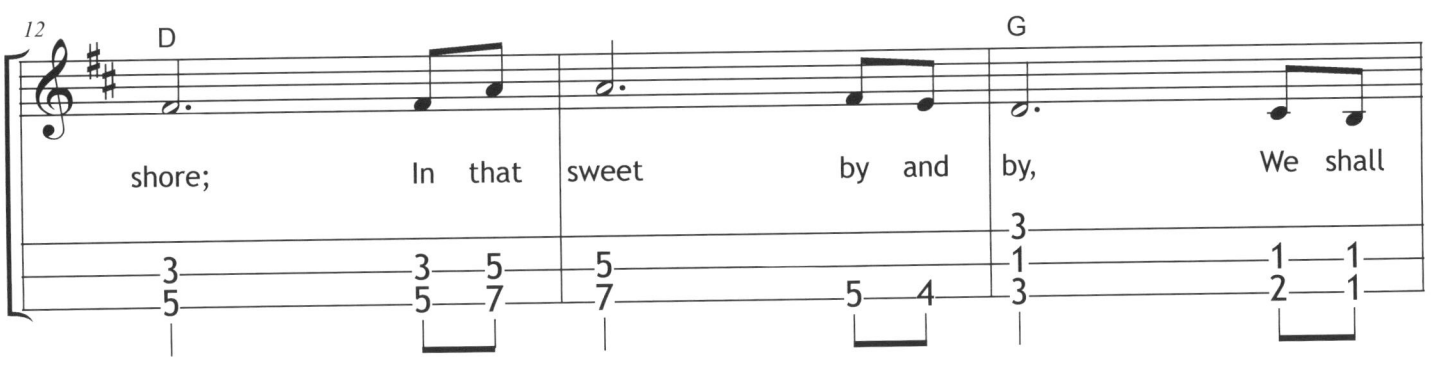

2. We shall sing on that beautiful shore,
The melodious songs of the blest,
And our spirits shall sorrow no more,
Not a sigh for the blessing of rest.
          Chorus

3. To our bountiful Father above,
We will offer our tribute of praise,
For the glorious gift of His love,
And the blessings that hallow our days.
          Chorus

Twilight is Falling

Arr. by Anne Lough

Unseld/Kieffer

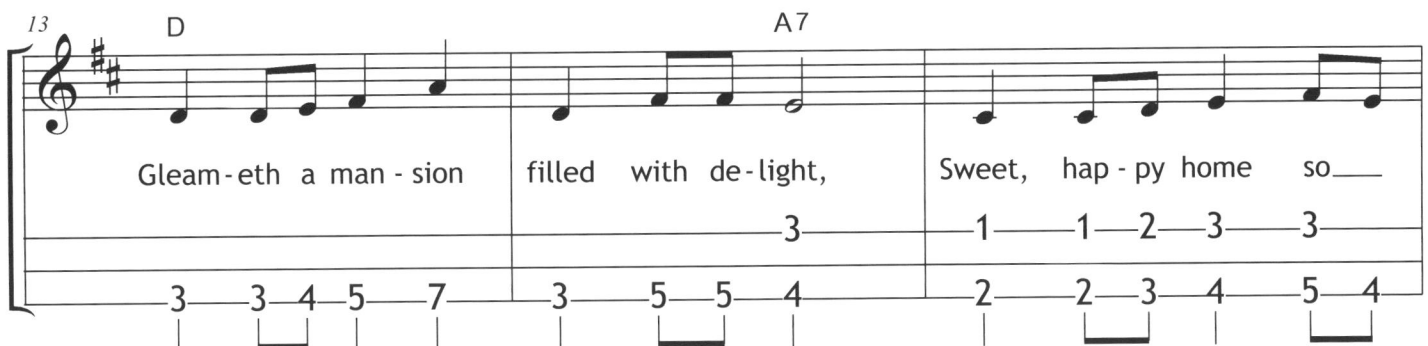

2. Voices of loved ones, songs of the past,
Still linger round me while life shall last;
Lonely I wander, sadly I roam,
Seeking that far-off home.
             Chorus

3. Come in the twilight, come, come to me,
Bringing some message over the sea;
Cheering my pathway while here I roam,
Seeking that far-off home.
             Chorus

Unclouded Day

Arr. by Anne Lough

Alwood

34

2. O they tell me of a home where my friends have gone,
O they tell me of that land far away,
Where the tree of life in eternal bloom
Sheds its fragrance through the unclouded day.
                Chorus

3. O they tell me of a King in His beauty there,
And they tell me that mine eyes shall behold
Where He sits on the throne that is whiter than snow,
In the city that is made of gold.
                Chorus

4. O they tell me that He smiles on His children there,
And His smile drives their sorrows all away;
And they tell me that no tears ever come again
In that lovely land of unclouded day.
                Chorus

What a Friend We Have in Jesus

Arr. by Anne Lough

Scriven/Converse

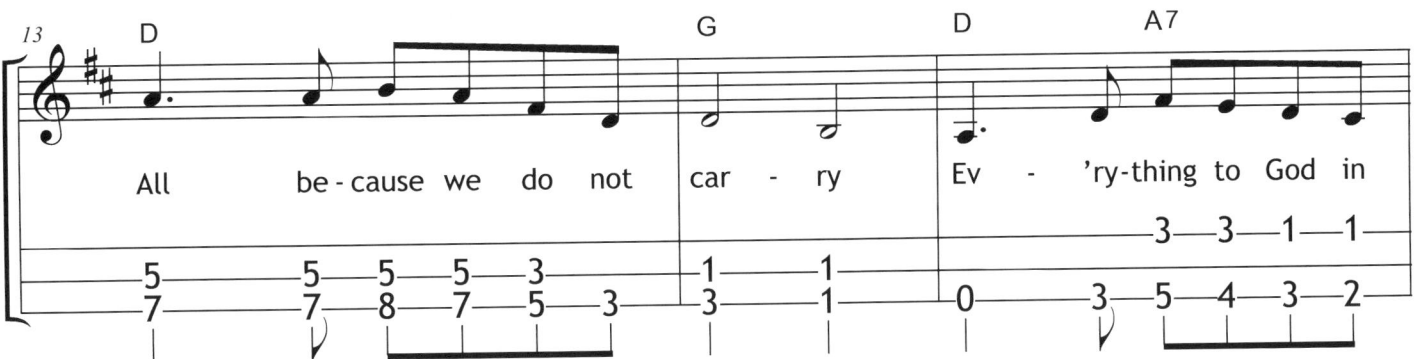

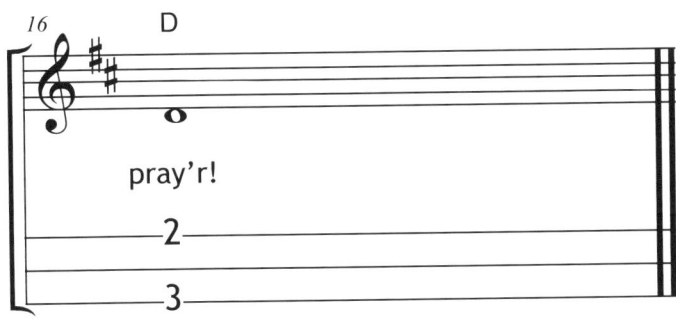

2. Have we trials and temptations? Is there trouble anywhere?
We should never be discouraged, Take it to the Lord in pray'r.
Can we find a friend so faithful Who will all our sorrows share?
Jesus knows our ev'ry weakness, Take it to the Lord in pray'r.

3. Are we weak and heavy laden, Cumbered with a load of care?
Precious Saviour, still our refuge, Take it to the Lord in pray'r.
Do thy friends despise, forsake thee? Take it to the Lord in pray'r;
In His arms He'll take and shield thee, Thou wilt find a solace there.

When the Roll is Called Up Yonder

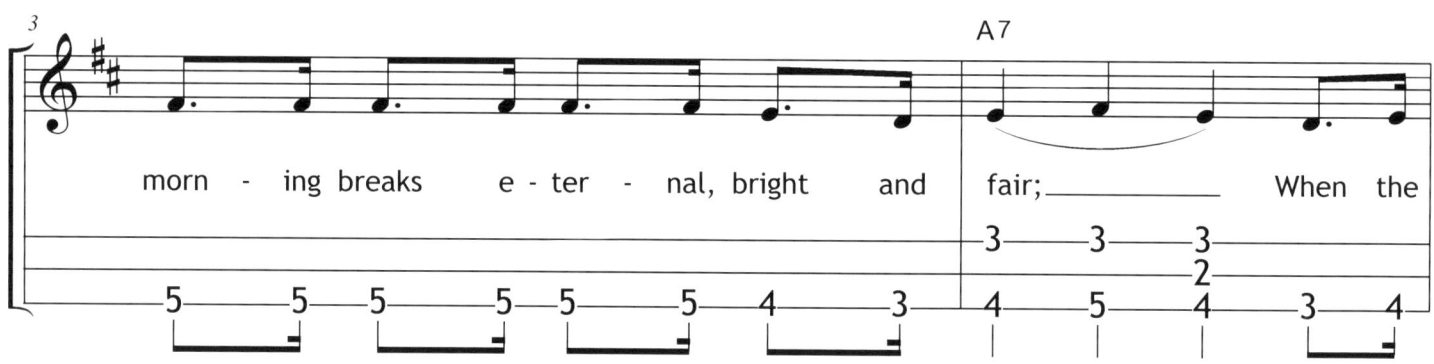
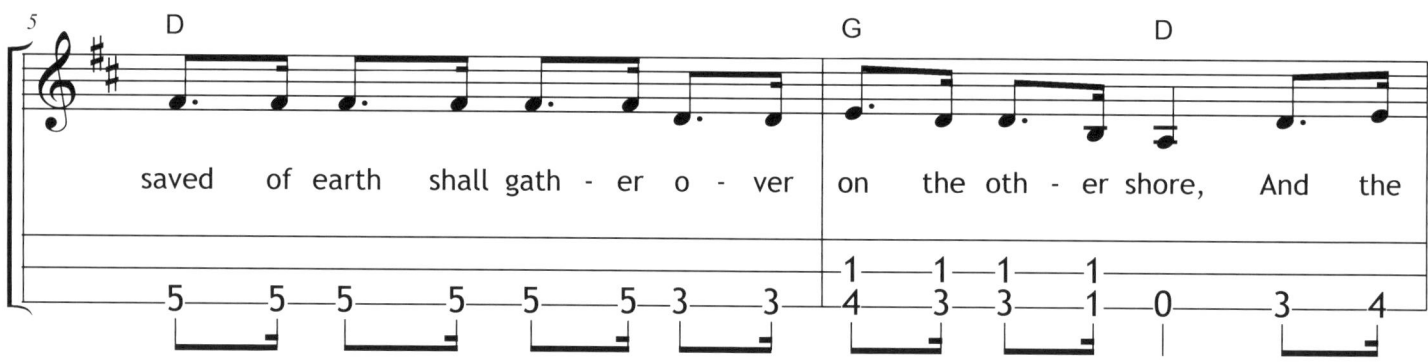
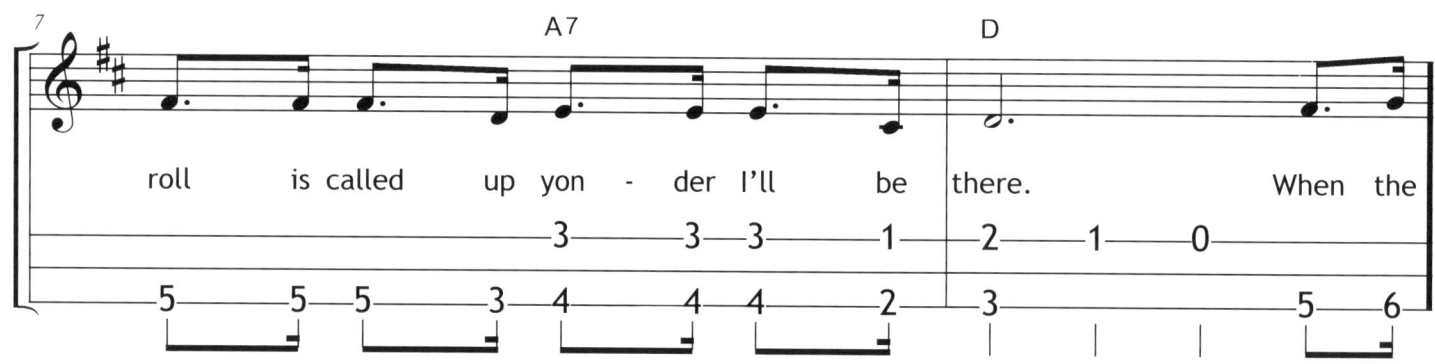

2. On that bright and cloudless morning when the dead in Christ shall rise,
And the glory of His resurrection share;
When His chosen ones shall gather to their home beyond the skies,
And the roll is called up yonder, I'll be there.
       Chorus

3. Let us labor for the Master from the dawn till setting sun,
Let us talk of all His wondrous love and care;
Then when all of life is over and our work on earth is done,
And the roll is called up yonder, I' ll be there.
       Chorus

The Mixolydian Mode or DAD

The **Mixolydian** mode or tuning is often referred to as **DAD**, **1-5-8** or **Do-Sol-Do** tuning. The **Mixoydian** mode is almost identical to the major mode, with the exception that the last step is a whole instead of a half. This has become a very popular tuning since the addition of the 6 1/2 fret. In **DAD** tuning it is possible to play traditional **Mixolydian** tunes, such as Old Joe Clark, using the 6th fret, or tunes in the major mode using the 6 1/2 fret. **DAD** is a nice tuning for fiddle tunes and melodies with a wide, high range. Notes that fall below the **Do** of the scale will need to be plucked on the middle, and sometimes the bass string.

To tune to this mode, keep the bass string tuned to **D** and the middle string tuned to **A**. The melody strings then will be tuned to **D** an octave higher than the bass string. This pitch can be sounded by plucking the bass string while holding it down on the 7th fret.

You are now tuned in **D Mixolydian (DAD)**. The starting point, or **Do**, of the scale is the open melody string. The **Mixolydian** scale would be played from the open to the 7th fret, using the 6th fret (skipping the 6 1/2). The major scale would be played from the open to the 7th fret substituting the 6 1/2 fret for the 6th. The intervals of the 0, 2nd, 4th and 7th frets outline the D, or I chord. As with the Ionian tuning, this tuning is based on the relationship of the 1st and 5th scale step, and could be pitched higher or lower tuning to the 1st, 5th and octave of the desired scale.

Blessed Assurance

Arr. by Anne Lough

Crosby/Knapp

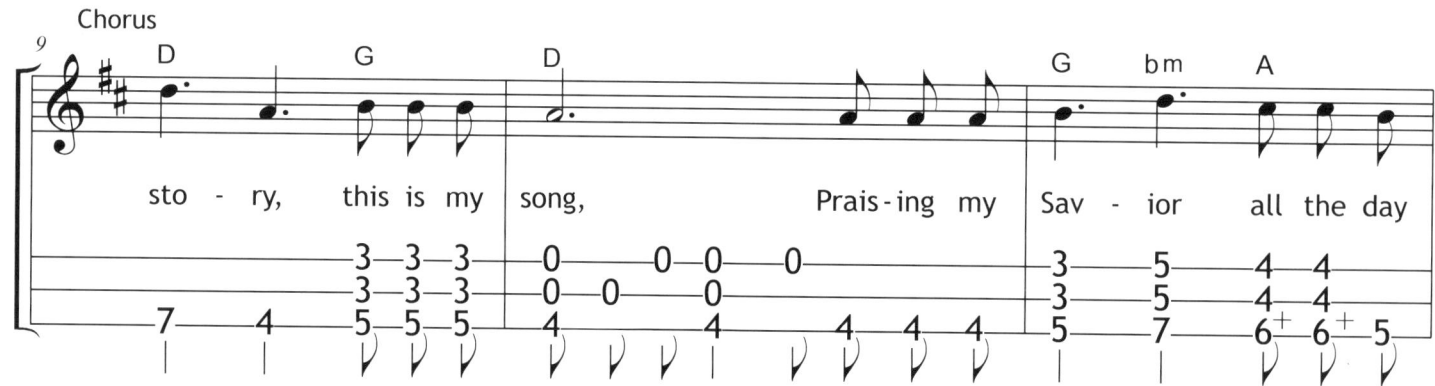

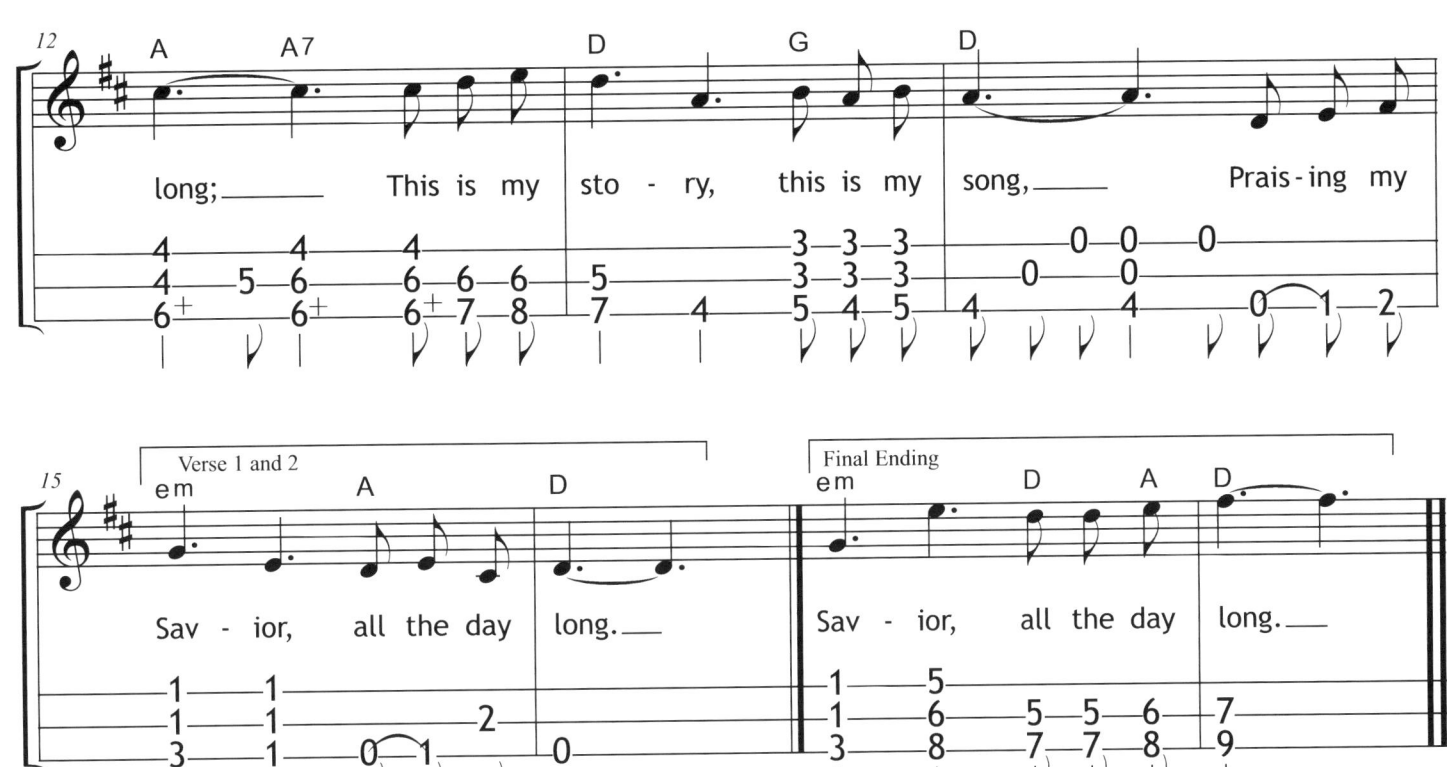

2. Perfect submission, perfect delight; Visions of rapture now burst on my sight; Angels descending bring from above Echoes of mercy, whispers of love.
                         Chorus

3. Perfect submission, all is at rest, I, in my Savior am happy and blest; Watching and waiting, looking above, Filled with His goodness, lost in His love.
                         Chorus

Come, Thou Fount of Every Blessing

Nettleton

Arr. by Anne Lough

Robert Robinson

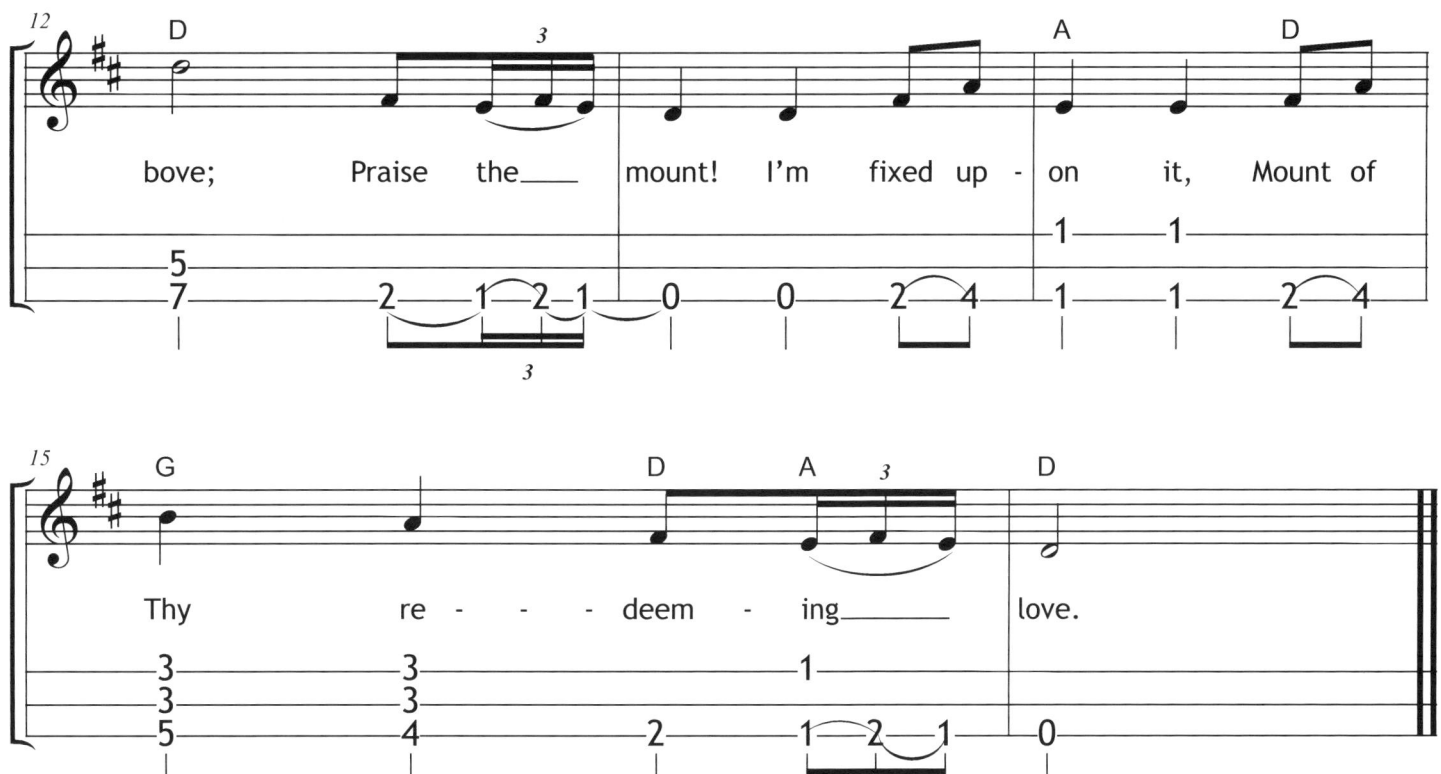

2. Here I raise my Ebenezer; Hither by Thy help I'm come;
And I hope, by Thy good pleasure, Safely to arrive at home.
Jesus sought me when a stranger, Wand'ring from the fold of God;
He, to rescue me from danger, Interposed His precious blood.

3. O to grace how great a debtor Daily I'm constrained to be!
Let Thy grace, Lord, like a fetter, Bind my wand'ring heart to Thee;
Prone to wander, Lord, I feel it, Prone to leave the God I love;
Here's my heart, Lord, take and seal it, Seal it for Thy courts above.

Come, Thou Fount of Every Blessing
Warrenton

Arr. by Anne Lough

Robert Robinson

2. Here I raise my Ebenezer; Hither by Thy help I'm come;
And I hope by Thy good pleasure Safely to arrive at home.
                Chorus

3. O, to grace how great a debtor Daily I'm constrained to be!
Let Thy grace, Lord, like a fetter, Bind my wand'ring heart to Thee.
                Chorus

Fairest Lord Jesus

Arr. by Anne Lough

Seiss/Willis

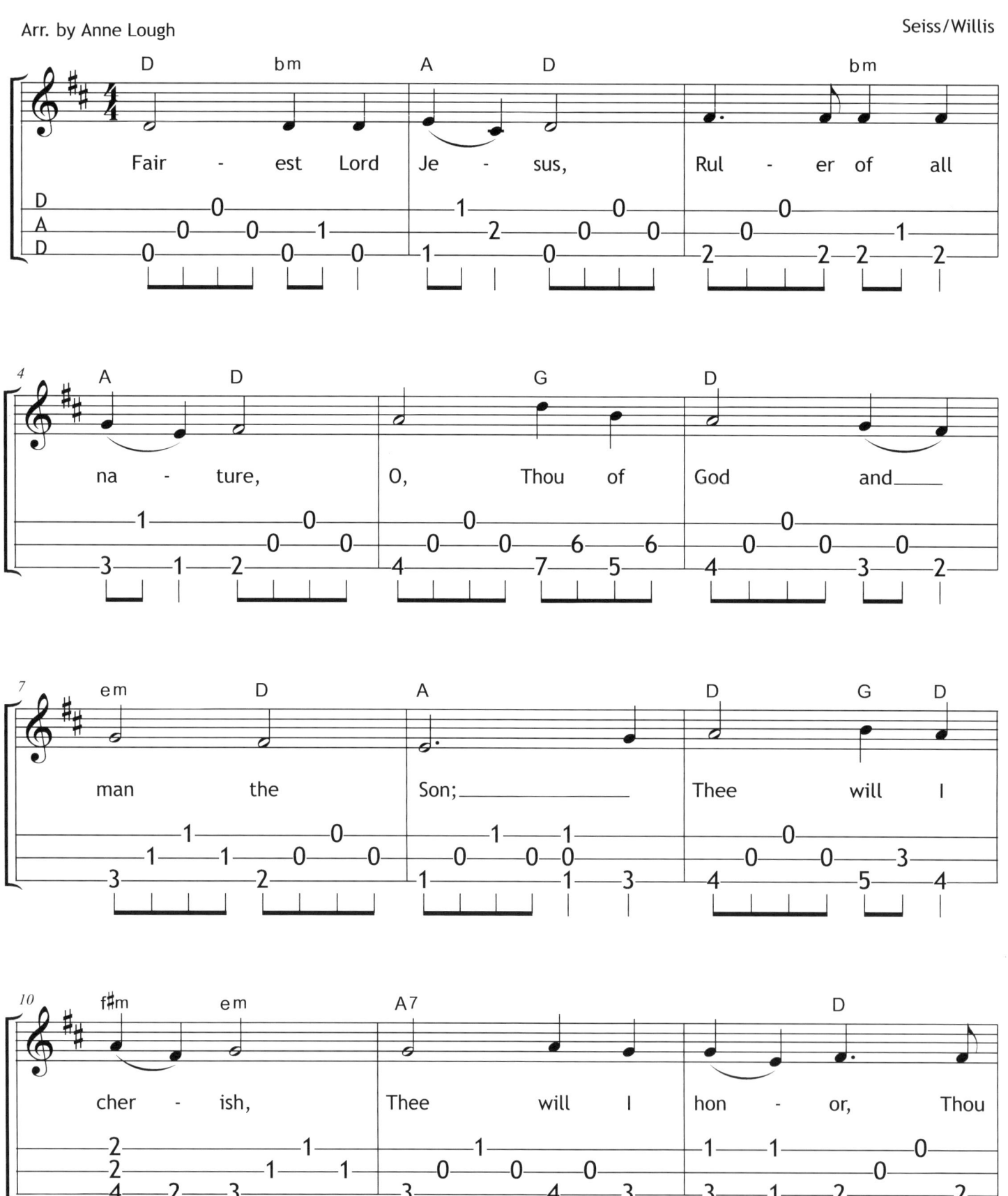

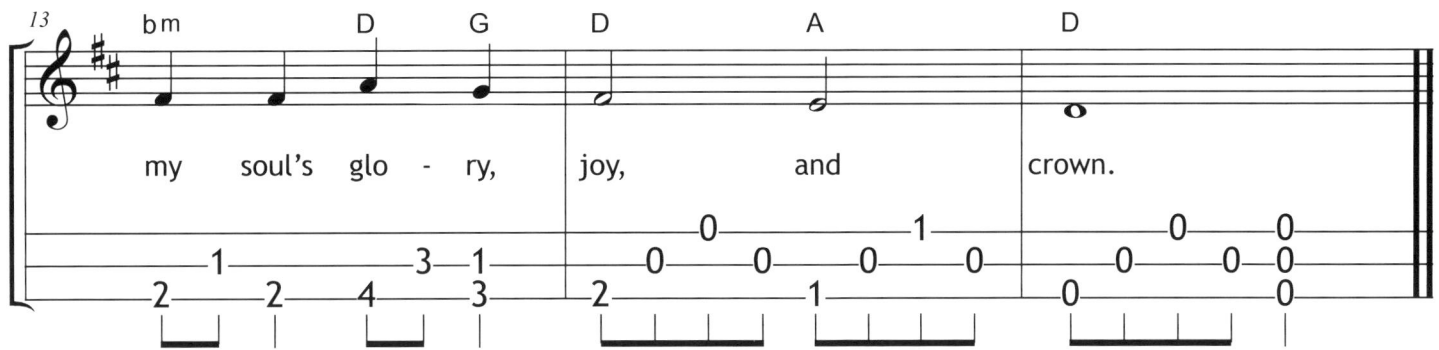

2. Fair are the meadows, Fairer still the woodlands,
Robed in the blooming garb of spring;
Jesus is fairer, Jesus is purer;
Who makes the woeful heart to sing.

3. Fair is the sunshine, Fairer still the moonlight
And all the twinkling, starry host;
Jesus shines brighter, Jesus shines purer
Than all the angels heav'n can boast.

4. Beautiful Saviour, Lord of all nations,
Son of God and Son of man!
Glory and honor, Praise, adoration,
Now and forevermore be Thine!

He Leadeth Me

Arr. by Anne Lough
Gilmore/Bradbury

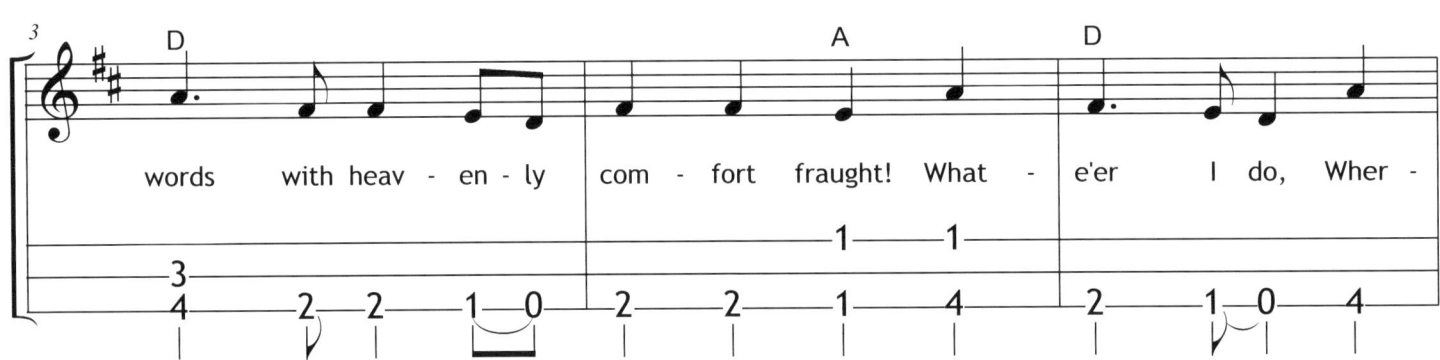
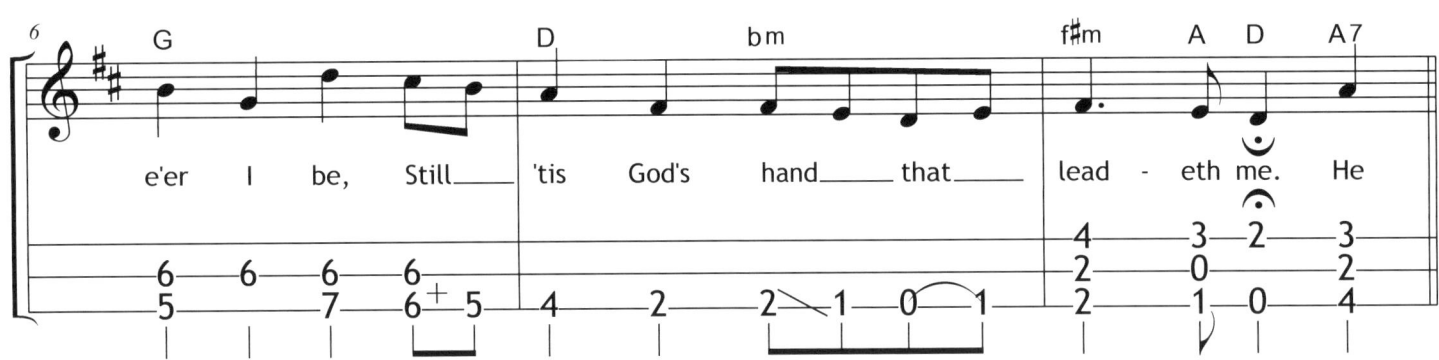
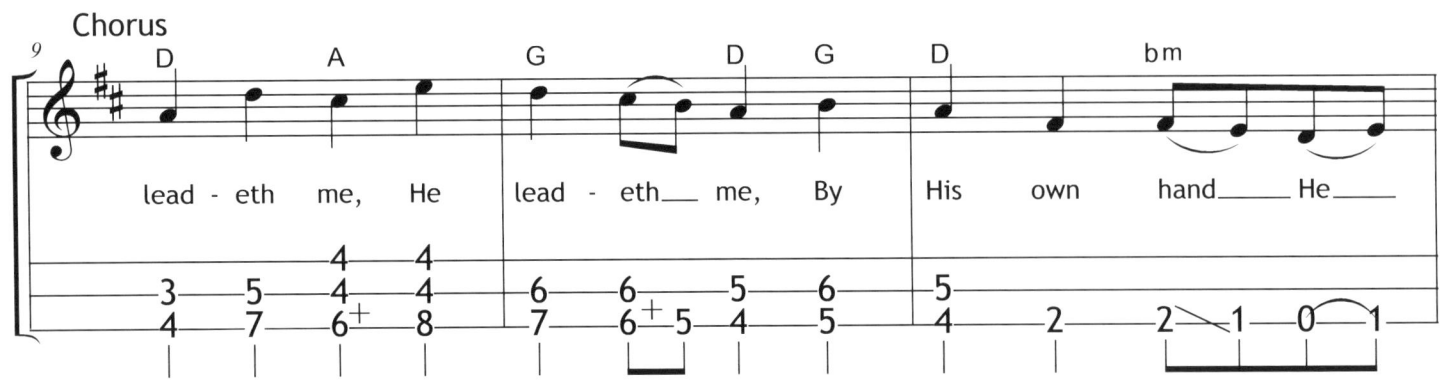

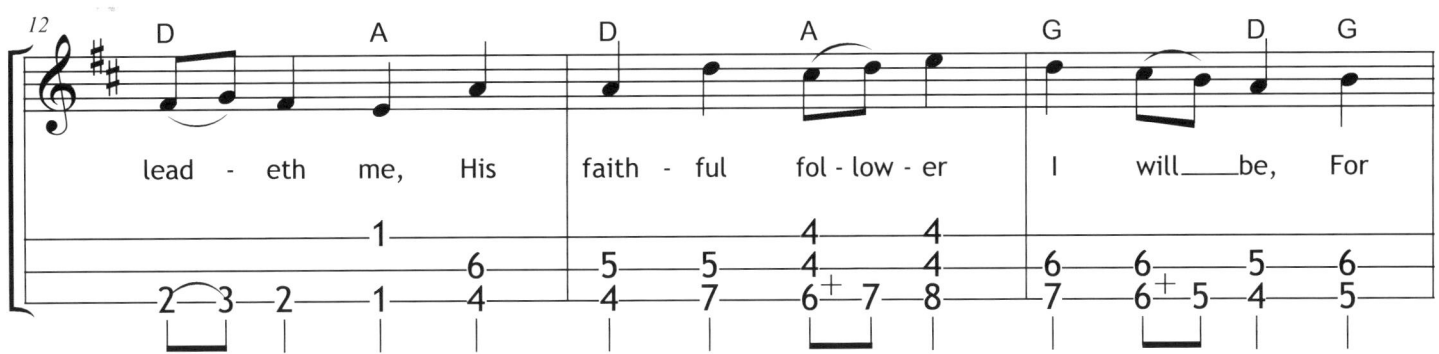
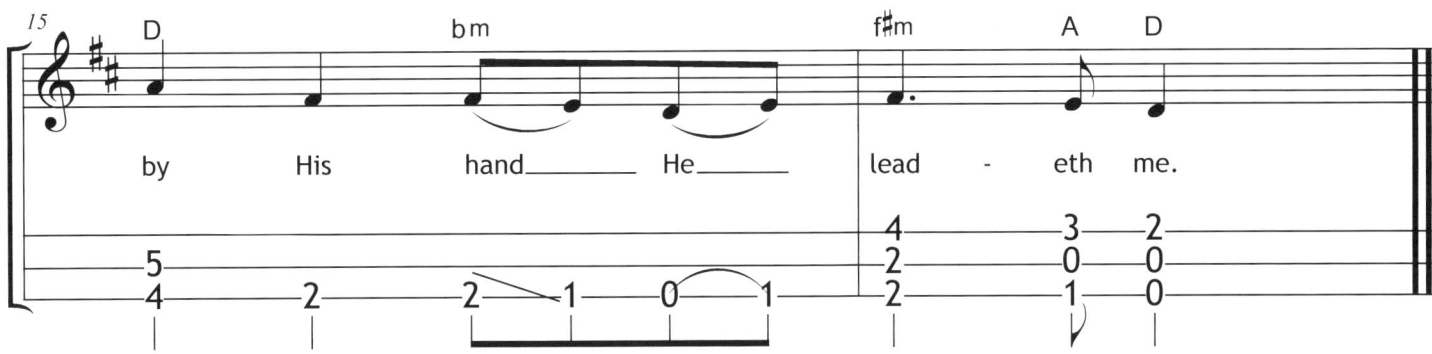

2. Sometimes mid scenes of deepest gloom, Sometimes where Eden's bowers bloom,
By waters still, over troubled sea, Still 'tis His hand that leadeth me.
                  Chorus

3. Lord, I would place my hand in Thine, Nor ever murmur nor repine;
Content, whatever lot I see, Since 'tis God's hand that leadeth me.
                  Chorus

4. And when my task on earth is done, when by Thy grace the vict'ry's won,
E'en death's cold wave I will not flee, Since God through Jordan leadeth me.
                  Chorus

Holy, Holy, Holy

Arr. by Anne Lough

Heber/Dykes

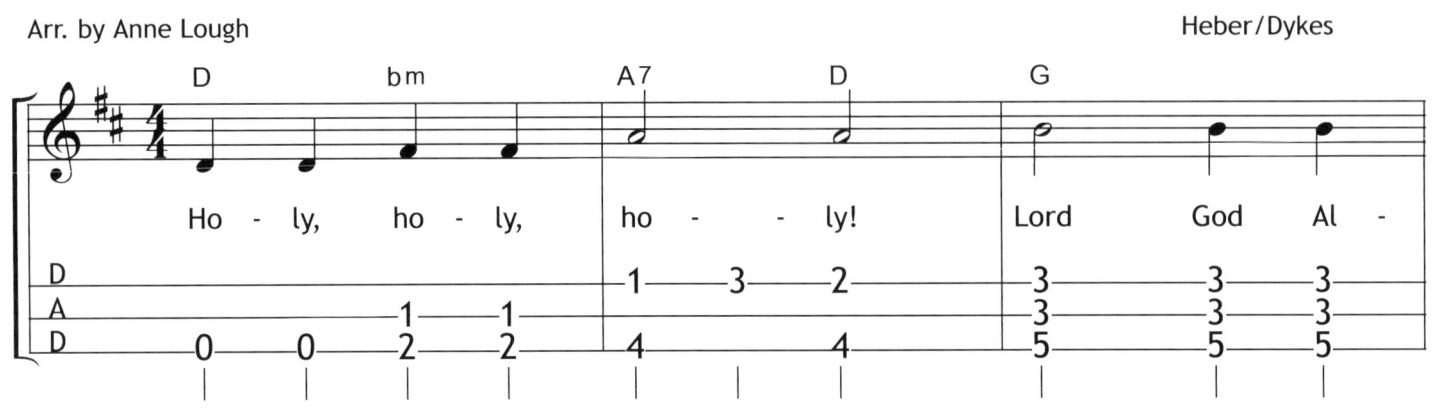
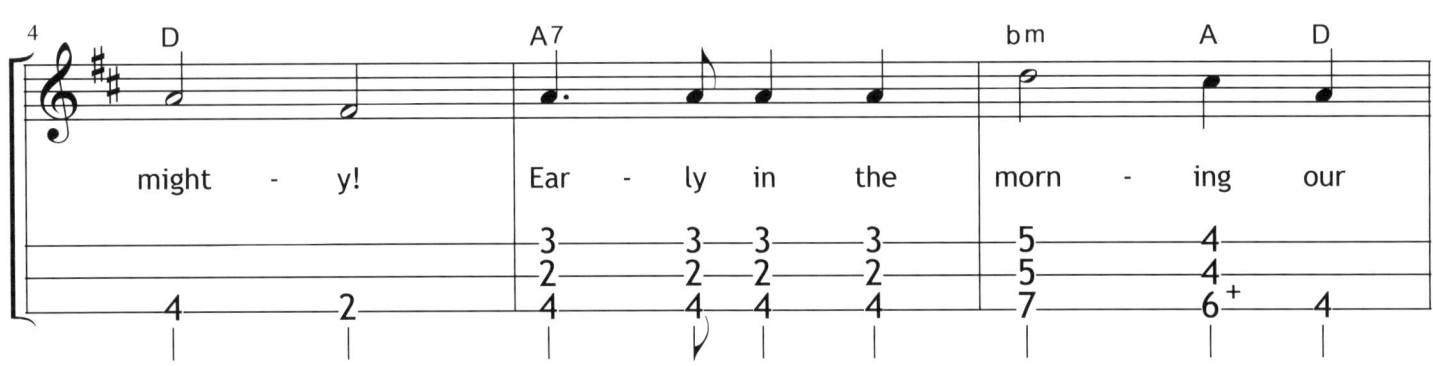
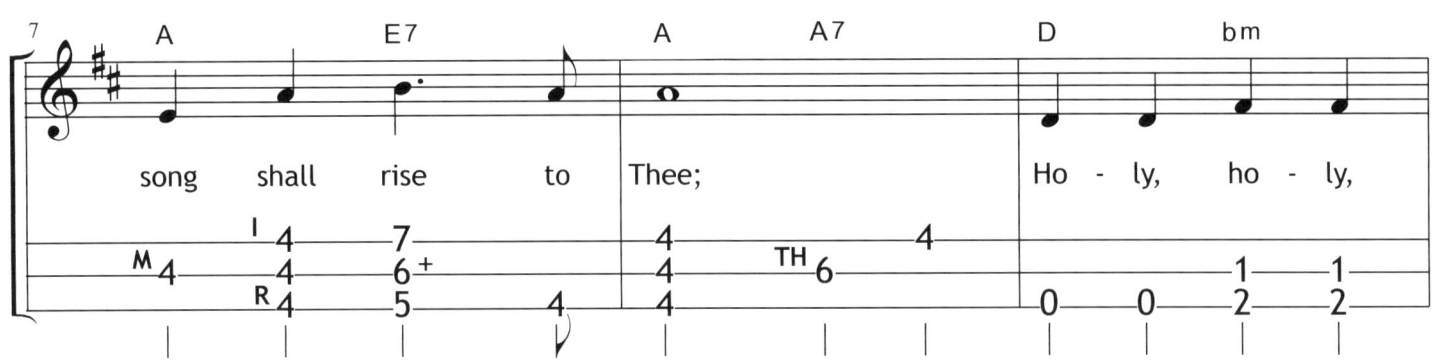
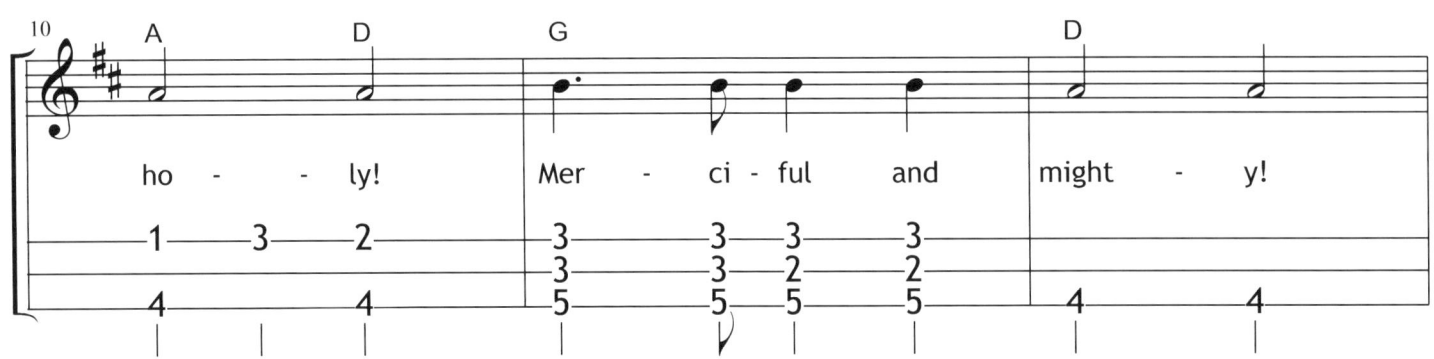

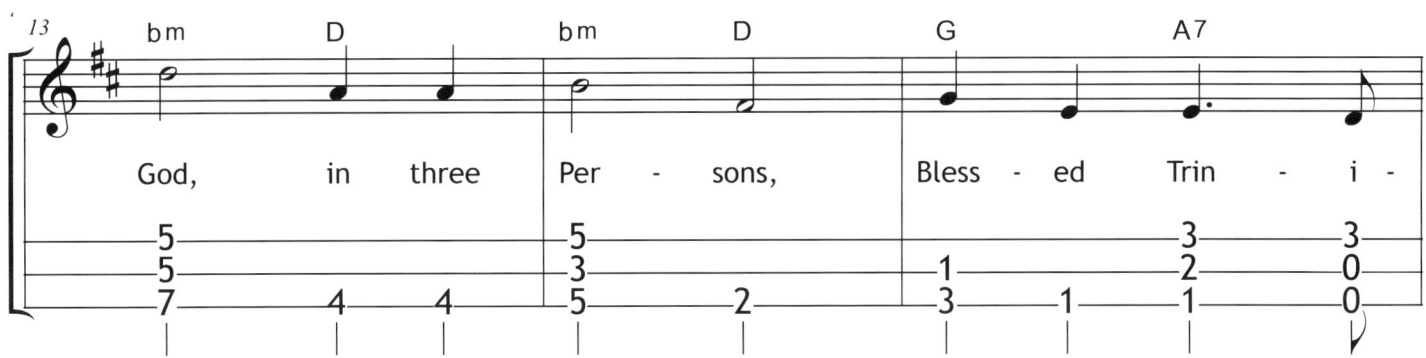

2. Holy, holy, holy! All the saints adore Thee,
Casting down their golden crowns around the glassy sea;
Cherubim and seraphim falling down before Thee,
Who wert, and art, and evermore shall be.

3. Holy, holy, holy! Tho the darkness hide Thee,
Tho the eye of sinful man Thy glory may not see;
Only Thou art holy, There is none beside Thee,
Perfect in pow'r, in love and purity.

4. Holy, holy, holy! Lord God Almighty!
All Thy works shall praise Thy name, in earth, and sky and sea;
Holy, holy, holy! Merciful and mighty!
God in three Persons, Blessed Trinity!

It Is Well With My Soul

Arr. by Anne Lough

Stafford/Bliss

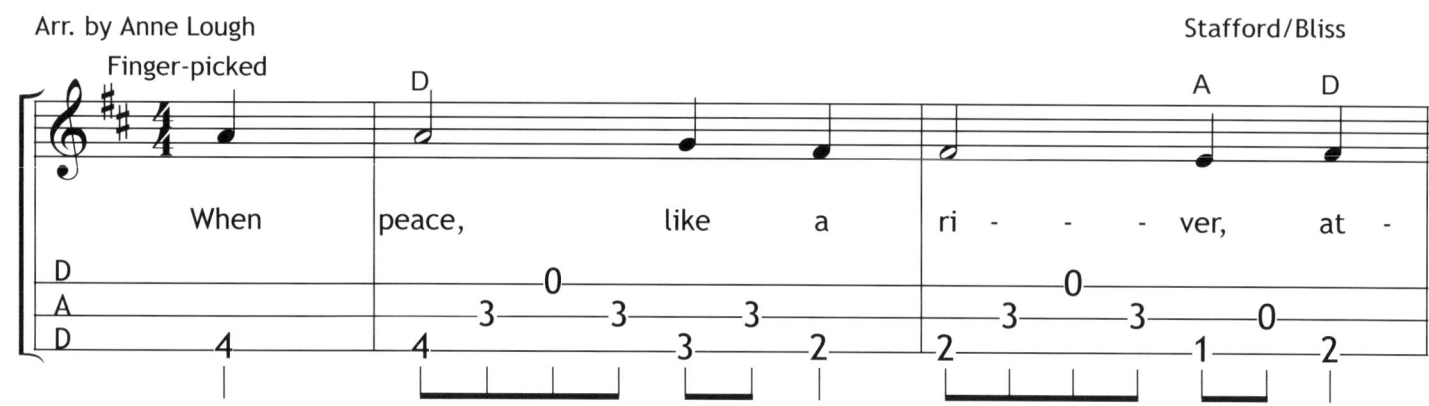
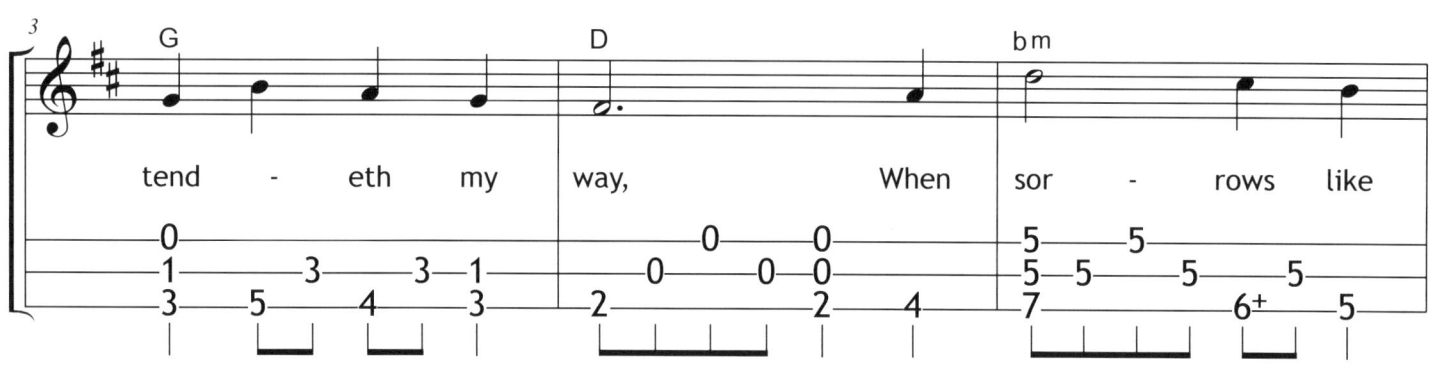
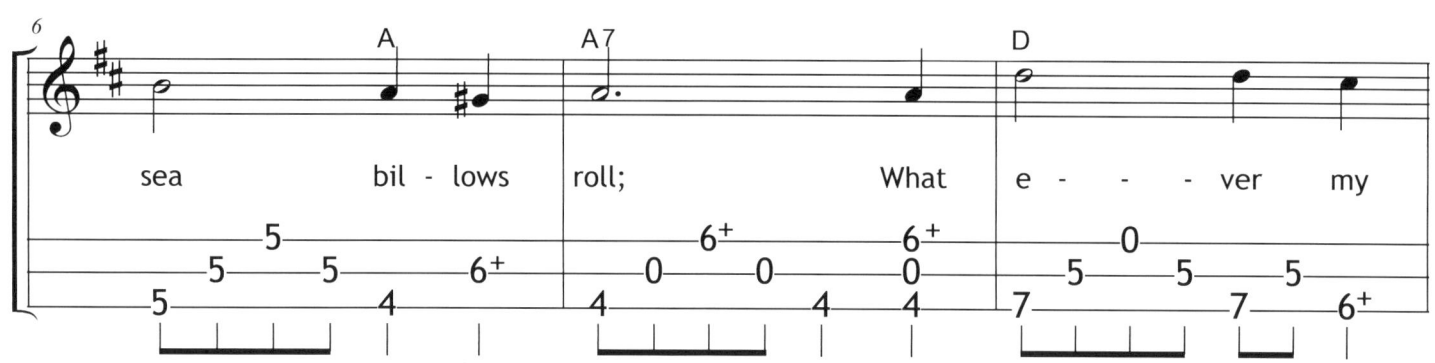
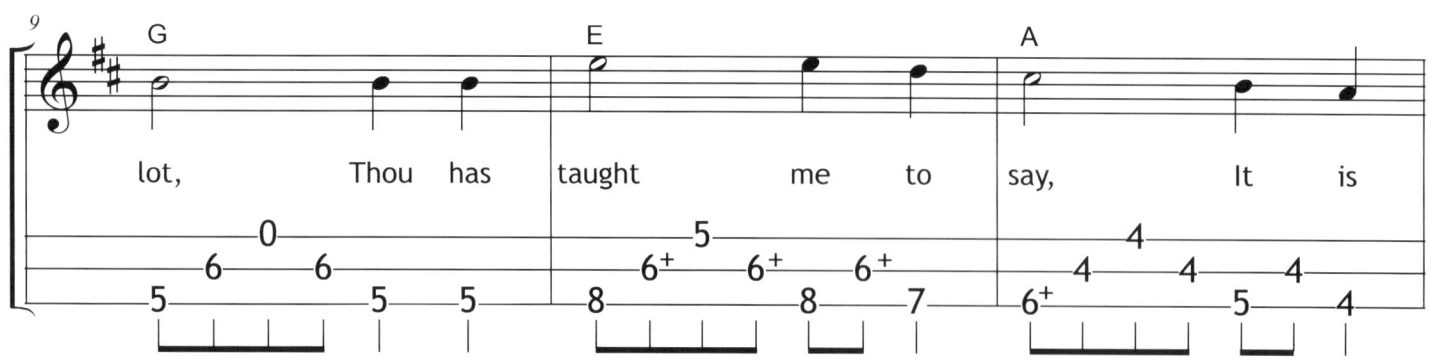

2. Tho Satan should buffet, tho trials should come, Let this blest assurance control,
That Christ has regarded my helpless estate, And hath shed His own blood for my soul.
Chorus

3. My sin, Oh, the bliss of this glorious tho't; My sin not in part, but the whole,
Is nailed to the cross and I bear it no more, Praise the Lord, praise the Lord, O my soul.
Chorus

4. And Lord, haste the day when the faith shall be sight, The clouds be rolled back as a scroll,
The trump shall resound and the Lord shall descend, "Even so," it is well with my soul.
Chorus

Just a Rose Will Do

As sung by Cleva Anderson
Brasstown, NC 1998

Arr. by Anne Lough

J.A. McClung

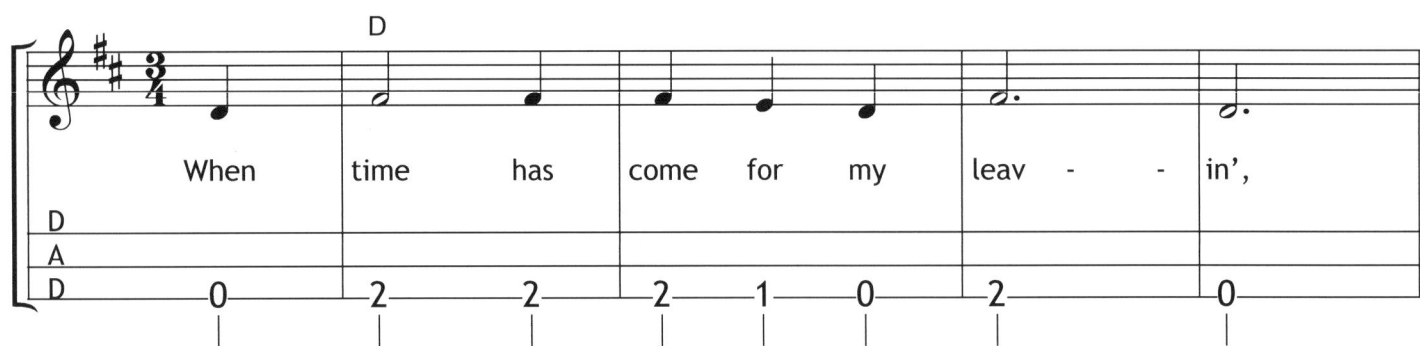

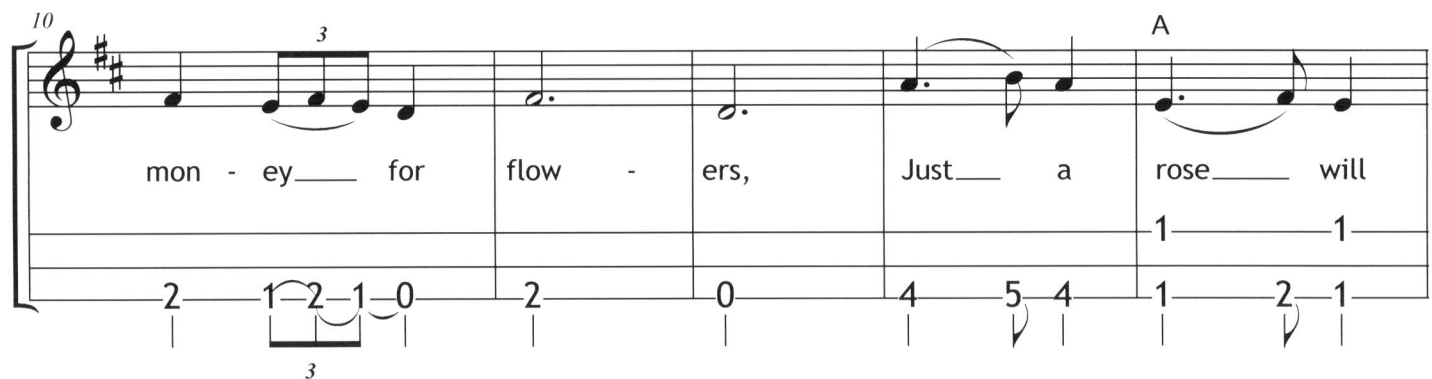
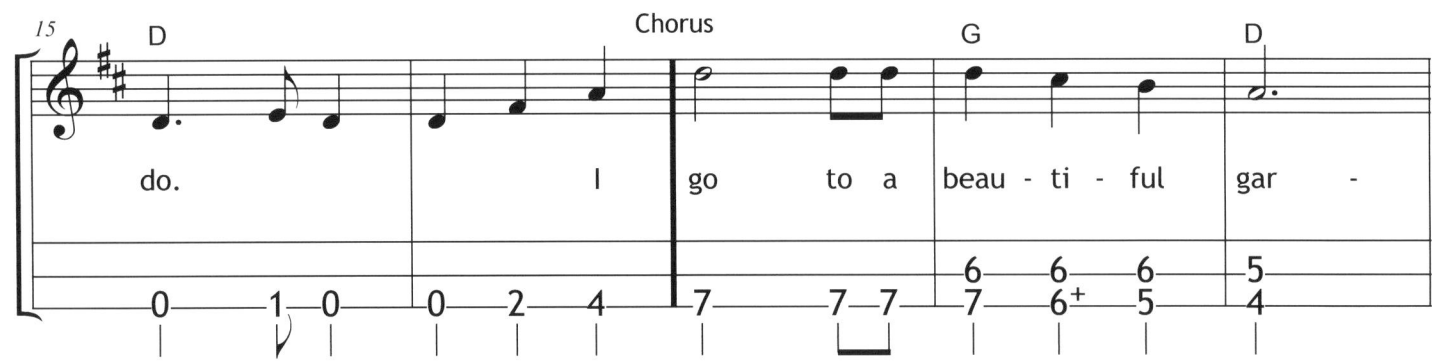

2. Just bring an old fashioned preacher,
To preach the gospel so true;
Don't want no fancy decorations,
Just a rose will do.
    Chorus

3. Don't want no weepin' or wailin',
When I come to that day;
Just want some old fashioned singin'
To help me on my way.
    Chorus

Just As I Am

Arr. by Anne Lough
Elliott/Bradbury

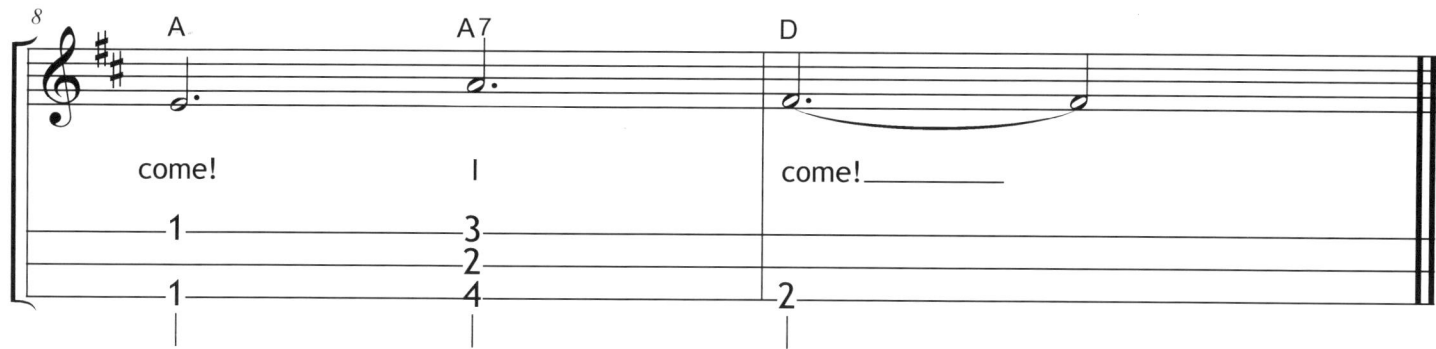

2. Just as I am, and waiting not, To rid my soul of one dark blot,
To Thee whose blood can cleanse each spot, O Lamb.....

3. Just as I am, tho tossed about, With many a conflict, many a doubt,
Fightings within and fears without, O Lamb.....

4. Just as I am, poor, wretched, blind, Sight, riches, healing of the mind,
Yea, all I need in Thee to find, O Lamb.....

5. Just as I am, Thou wilt receive, Wilt welcome, pardon, cleanse, relieve,
Because Thy promise I believe, O Lamb.....

6. Just as I am, Thy love unknown, Hath broken ev'ry barrier down,
Now to be Thine, yea Thine alone, O Lamb.....

Sweet Hour of Prayer

Arr. by Anne Lough
Walford/Bradbury

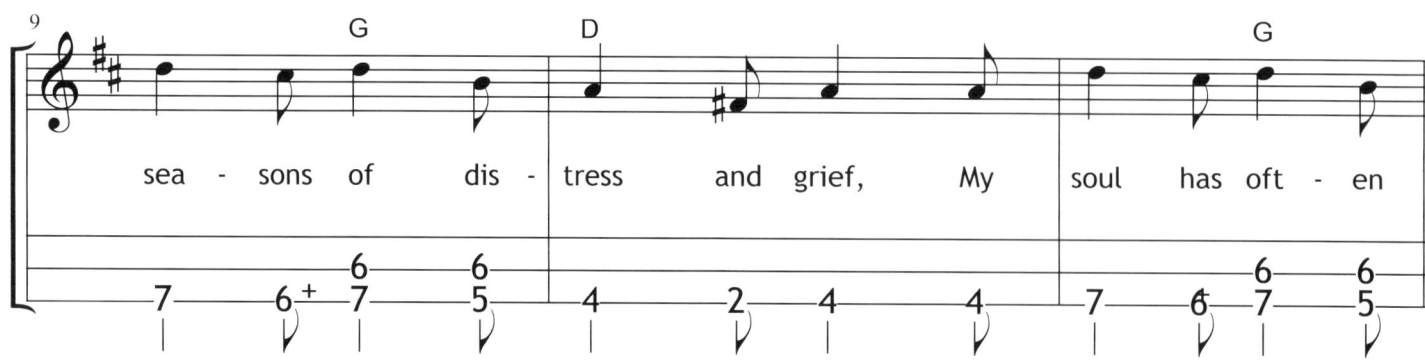

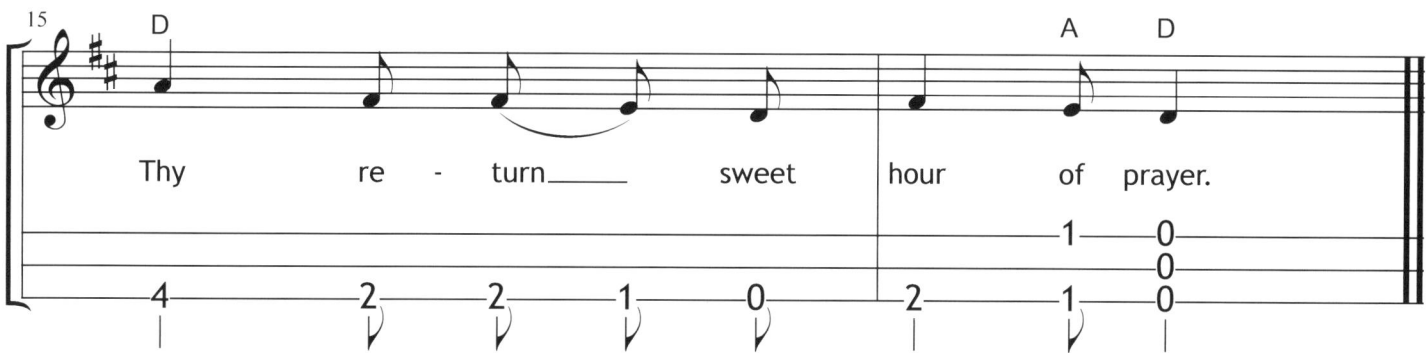

2. Sweet hour of prayer, sweet hour of prayer, Thy wings shall my petition bear,
To Him whose truth and faithfulness Engage my waiting soul to bless;
And since He bids me seek His face, Believe His word and trust His grace,
I'll cast on Him my ev'ry care, And wait for Thee, sweet hour of prayer.

3. Sweet hour of prayer, sweet hour of prayer, May I Thy consolation share,
Till, from Mount Pisgah's lofty height, I view my home and take my flight;
This robe of flesh I'll drop and rise To seize the everlasting prize;
And shout while passing thro' the air, "Farewell, farewell, sweet hour of prayer!"

Sweet Hour of Prayer

Arr. by Anne Lough
Walford/Bradbury

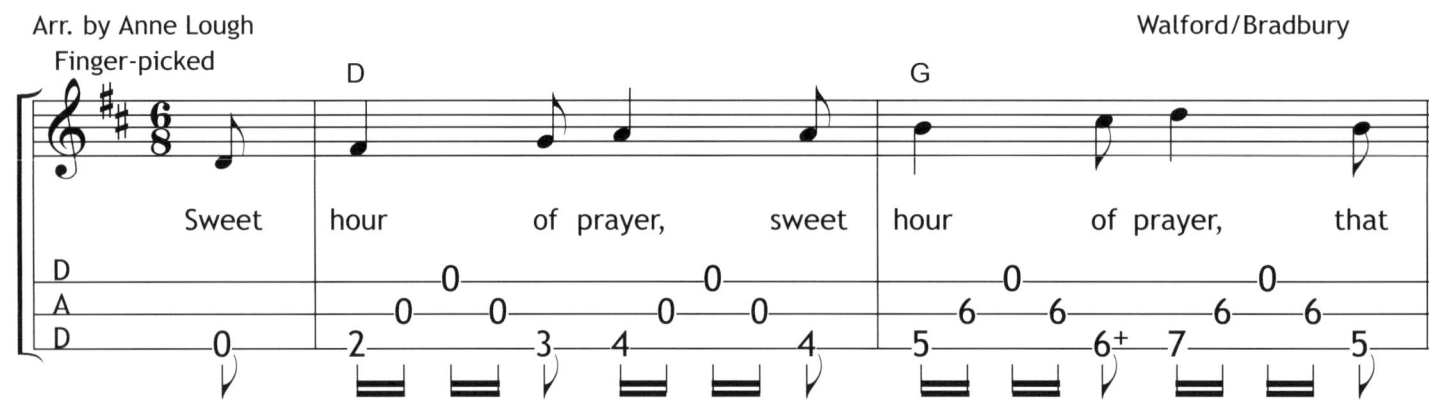
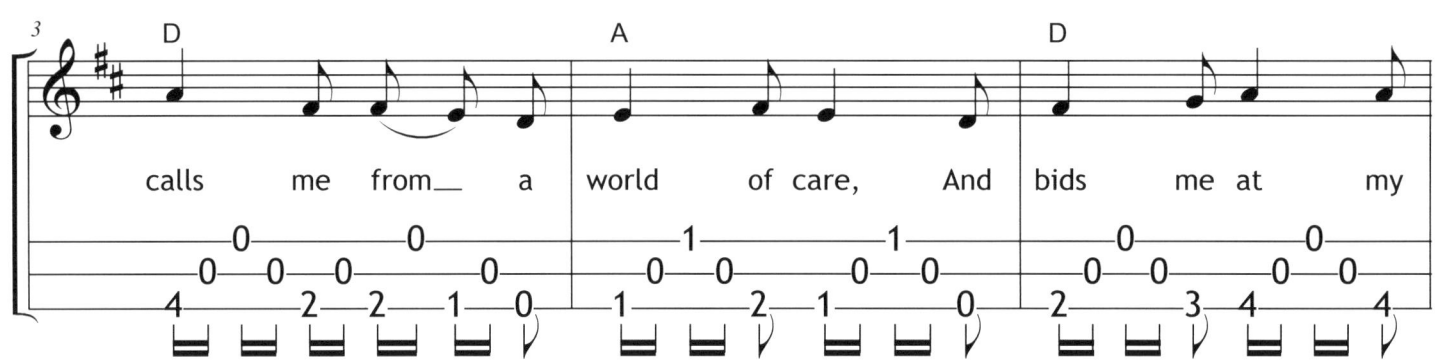
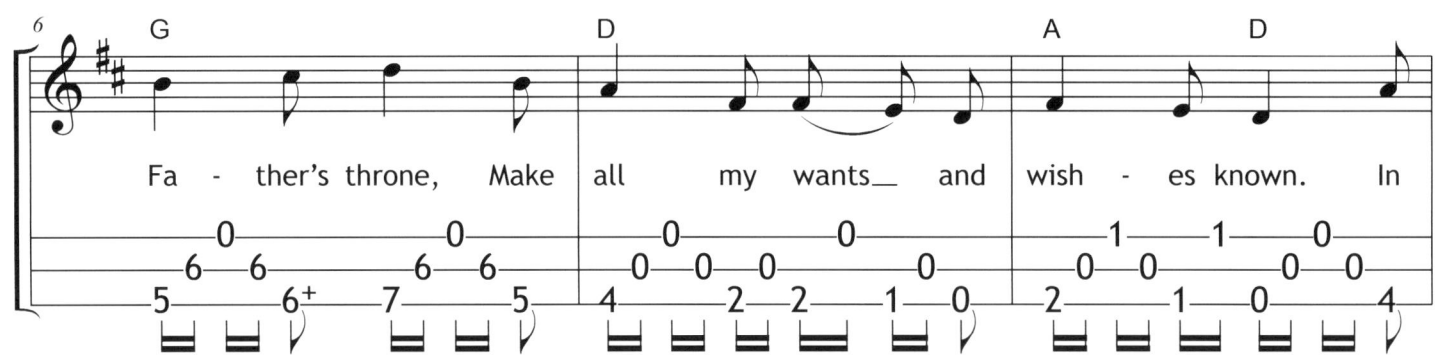
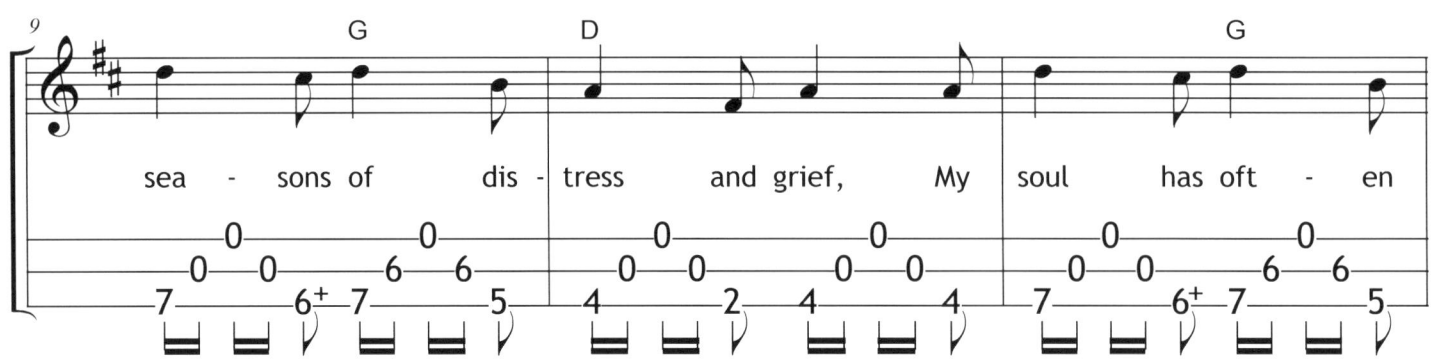

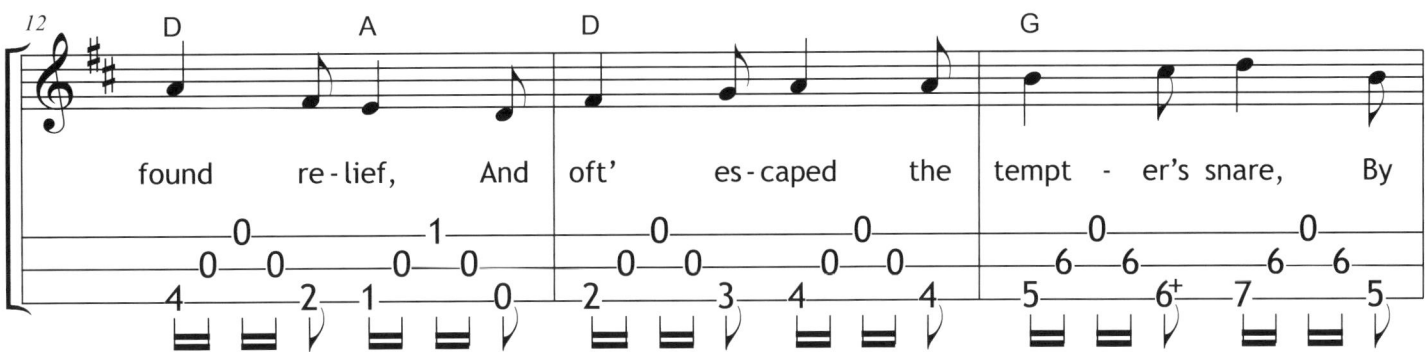
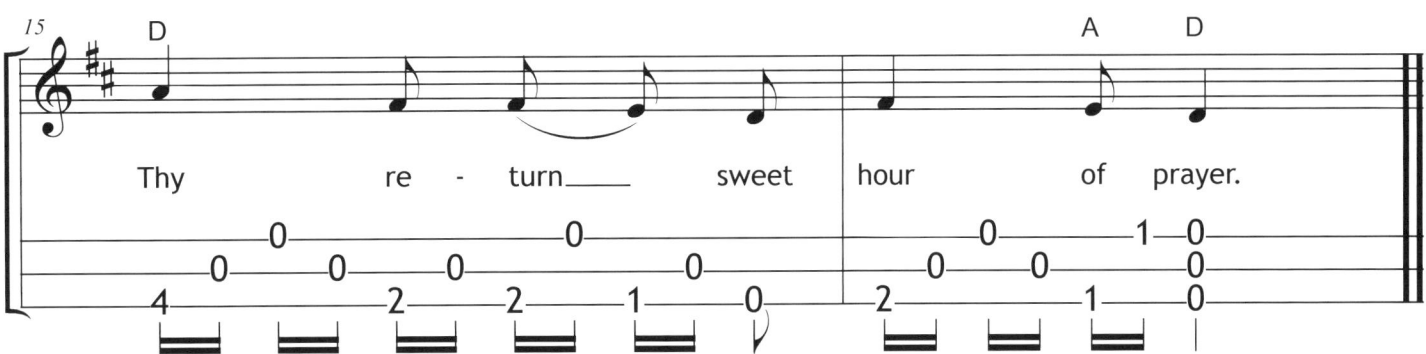

2. Sweet hour of prayer, sweet hour of prayer, Thy wings shall my petition bear,
To Him whose truth and faithfulness Engage my waiting soul to bless;
And since He bids me seek His face, Believe His word and trust His grace,
I'll cast on Him my ev'ry care, And wait for Thee, sweet hour of prayer.

3. Sweet hour of prayer, sweet hour of prayer, May I Thy consolation share,
Till, from Mount Pisgah's lofty height, I view my home and take my flight;
This robe of flesh I'll drop and rise To seize the everlasting prize;
And shout while passing thro' the air, "Farewell, farewell, sweet hour of prayer!"

There Is A Fountain

Arr. by Anne Lough
Cowper

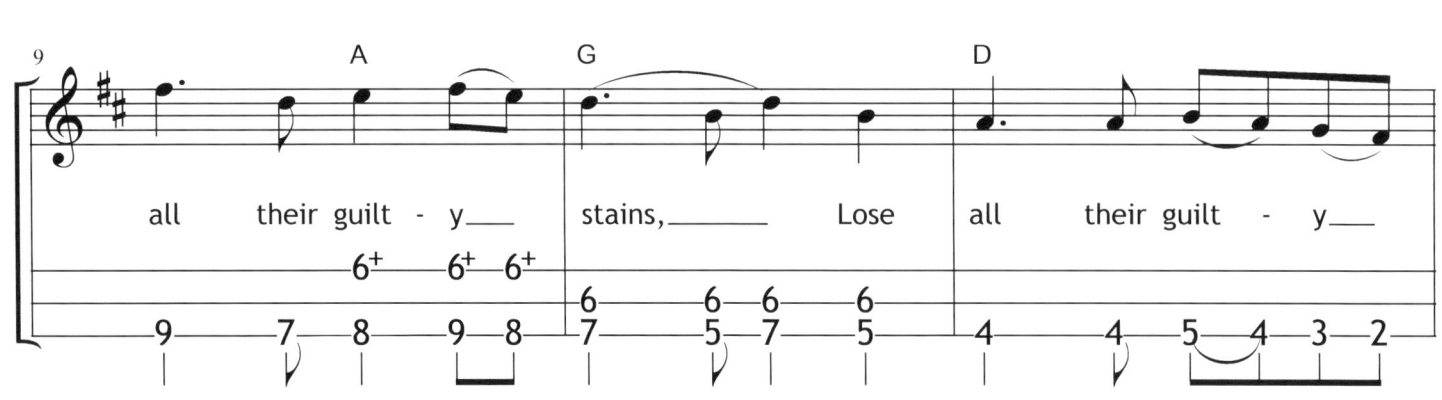

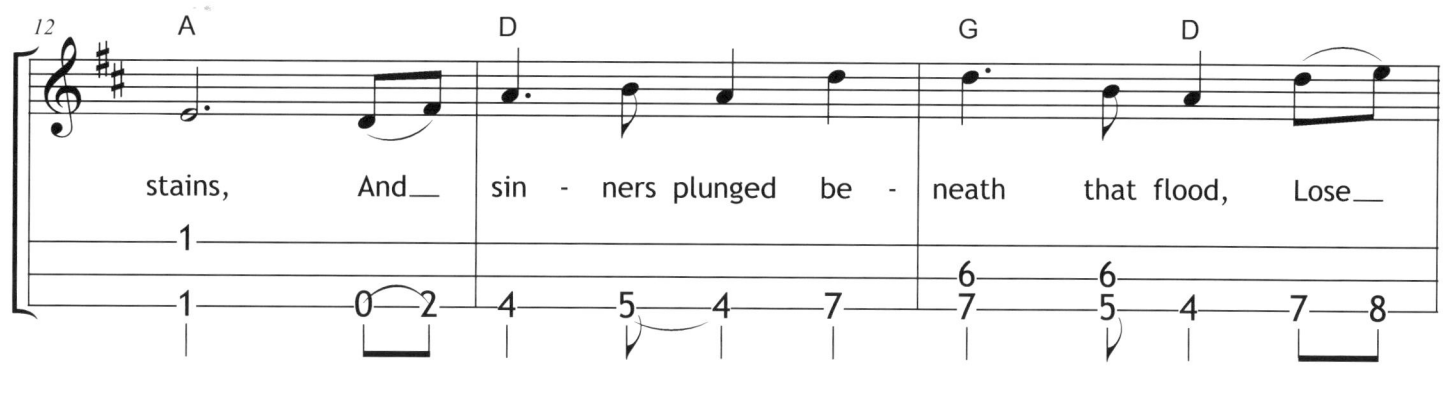
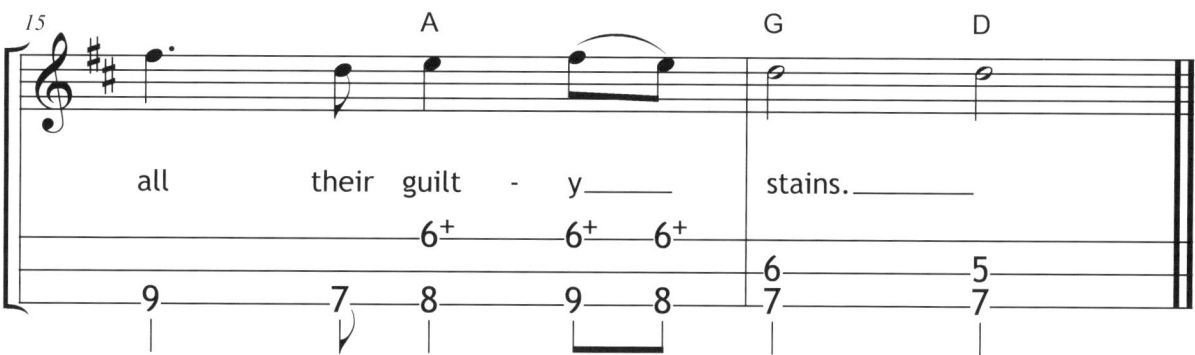

2. The dying thief rejoiced to see That fountain in His day;
And there may I, though vile as he, Wash all my sins away;
Wash all my sins away, Wash all my sins away,
And there may I, though vile as he, Wash all my sins away.

3. Dear dying Lamb, Thy precious blood Shall never lose its pow'r
Till all the ransomed church of God Be saved, to sin no more;
Be saved, to sin no more, Be saved, to sin no more;
Till all the ransomed church of God Be saved, to sin no more.

4. E'er since by faith I saw the stream Thy flowing wounds supply,
Redeeming love has been my theme, And shall be till I die;
And shall be till I die, And shall be till I die,
Redeeming love has been my theme, And shall be till I die.

Trust and Obey

Arr. by Anne Lough

Sammis/Tower

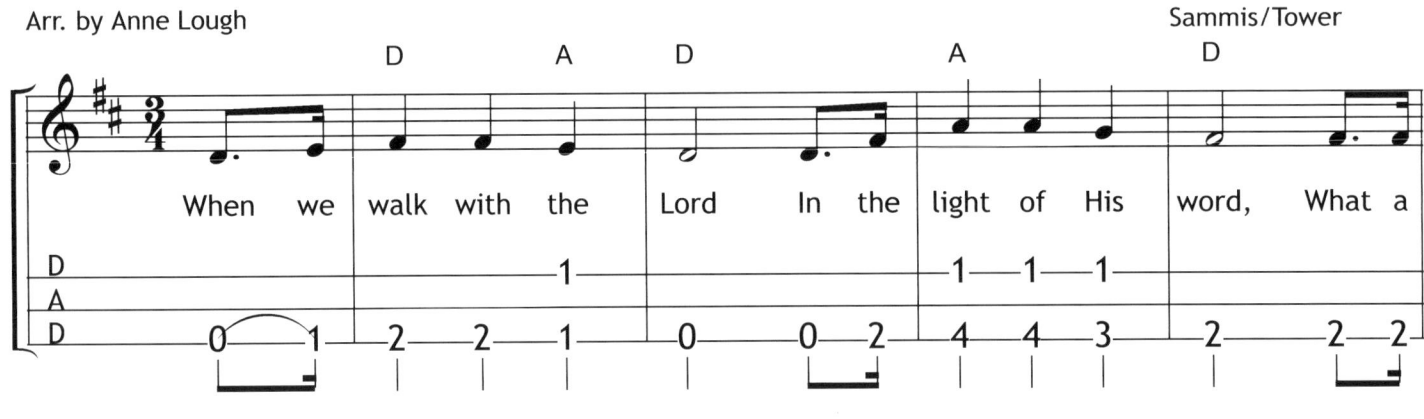
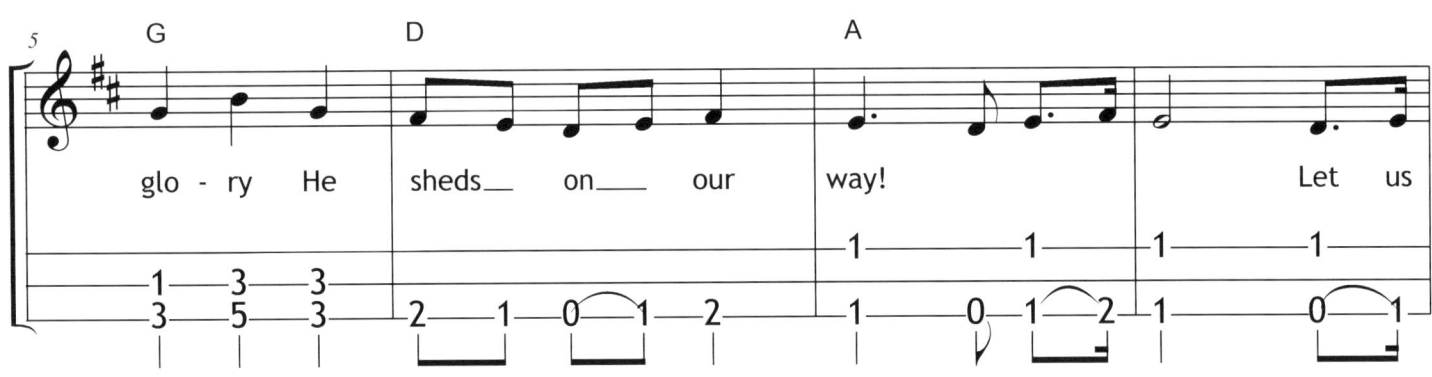
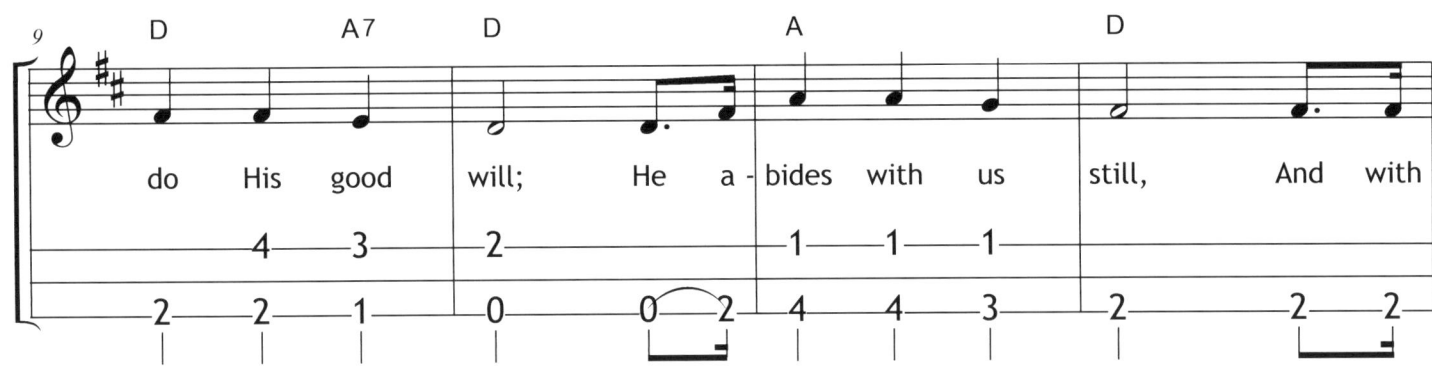
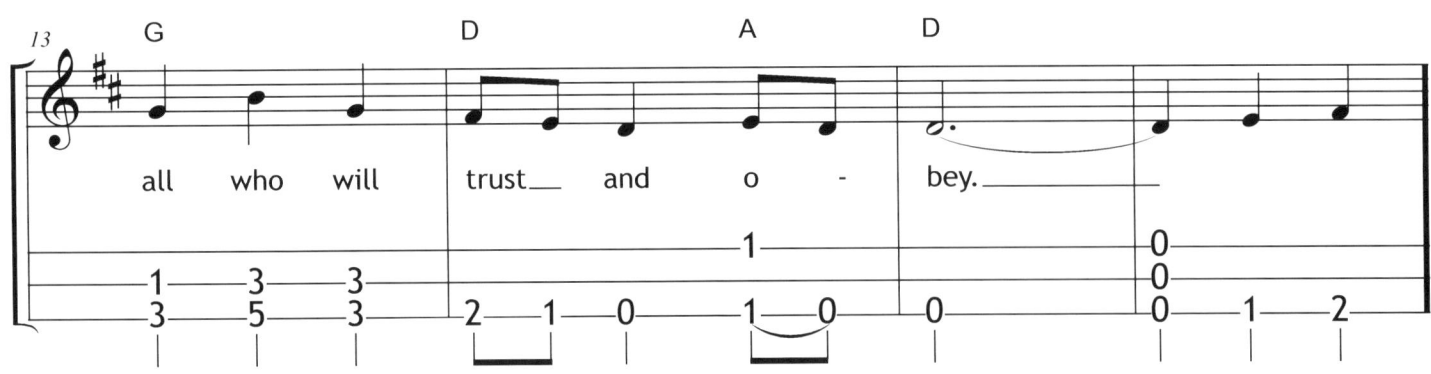

2. Not a burden we bear, Not a sorrow we share,
But our toil He doth richly repay;
Not a grief or a loss, Not a frown or a cross,
But is blest if we trust and obey.
              Chorus

3. But we never can prove The delights of His love
Until all on the alter we lay;
For the favor He shows And the joy He bestows
Are for them who will trust and obey.
              Chorus

4. Then in fellowship sweet We will sit at His feet,
Or we'll walk by His side in the way;
What He says we will do, Where He sends we will go;
Never fear, only trust and obey.
              Chorus

Were You There

Arr. by Anne Lough

African American Spiritual

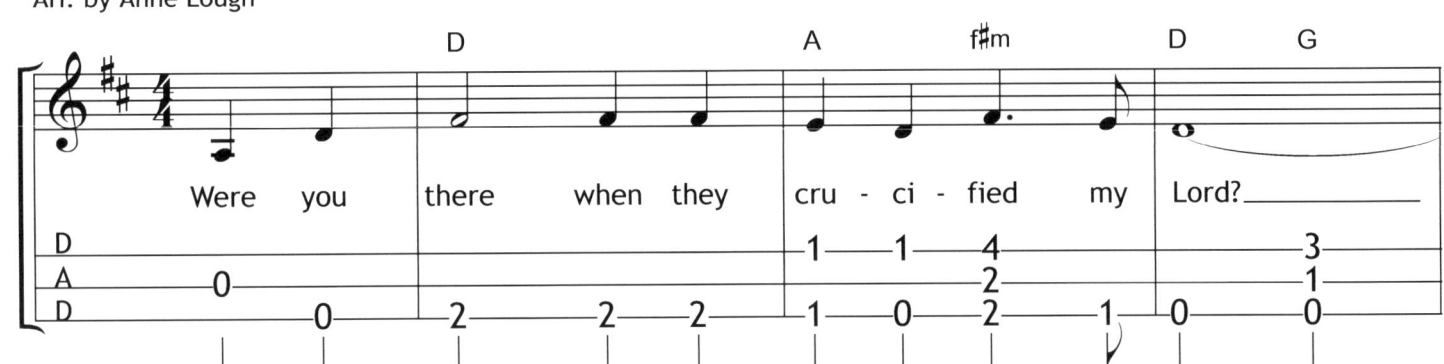
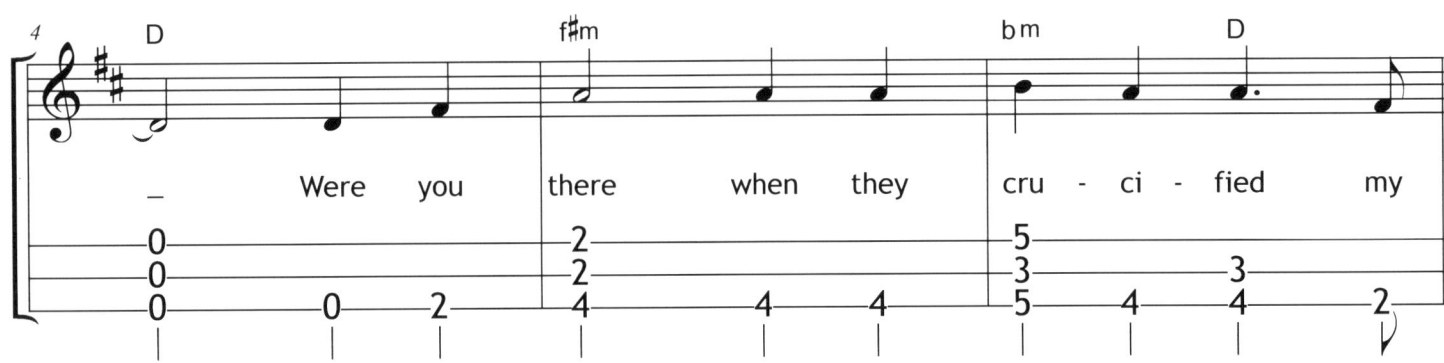
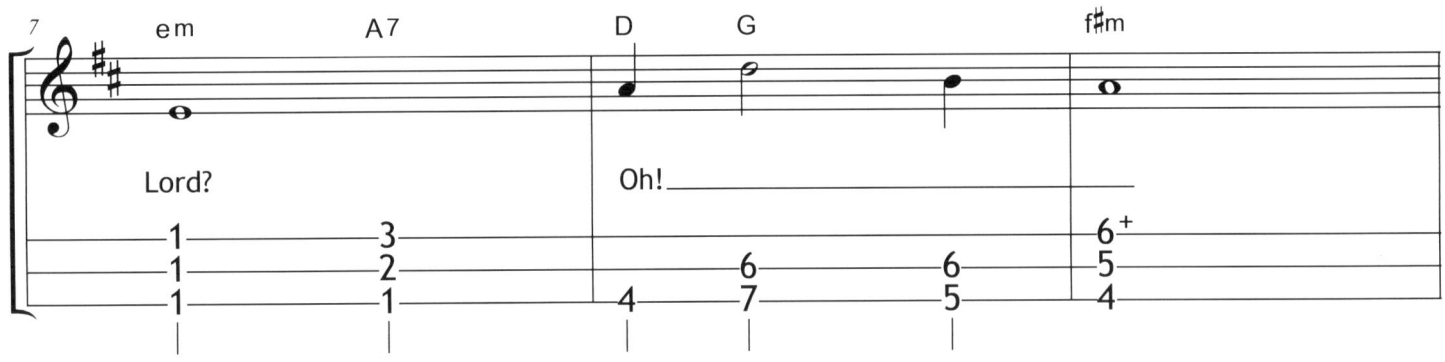

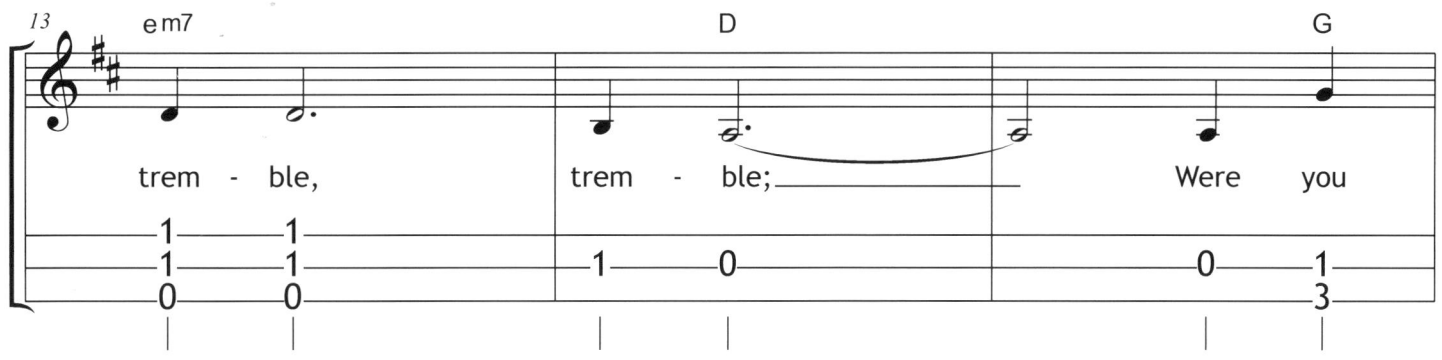
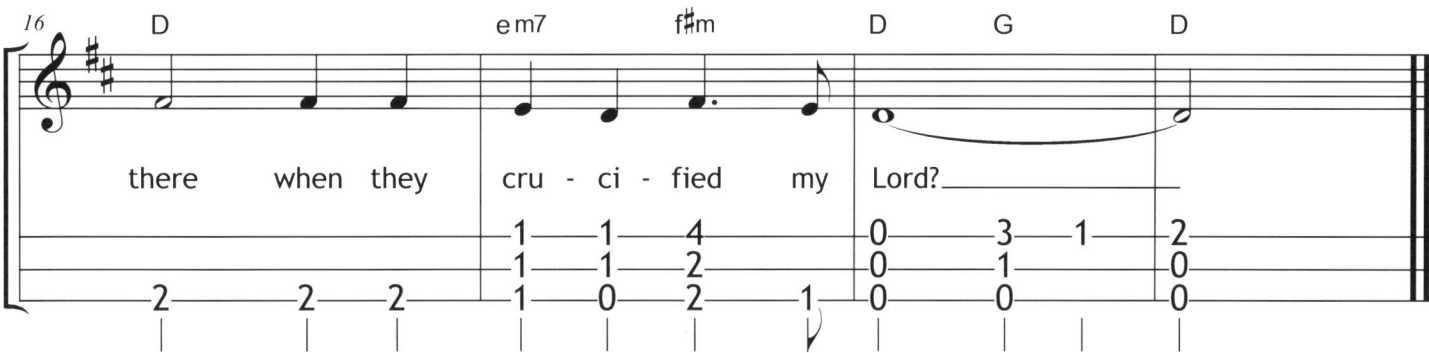

2. Were you there when they nailed Him to the tree?
Were you there when they nailed Him to the tree?
Oh! Sometimes it causes me to tremble, tremble, tremble;
Were you there when they nailed Him to the tree?

3. Were you there when they laid Him in the tomb?
Were you there when they laid Him in the tomb?
Oh! Sometimes it causes me to tremble, tremble, tremble;
Were you there when they laid Him in the tomb?

4. Were you there when He rose up from the grave?
Were you there when He rose up from the grave?
Oh! Sometimes it causes me to tremble, tremble, tremble;
Were you there when He rose up from the grave?

When the Morning Comes

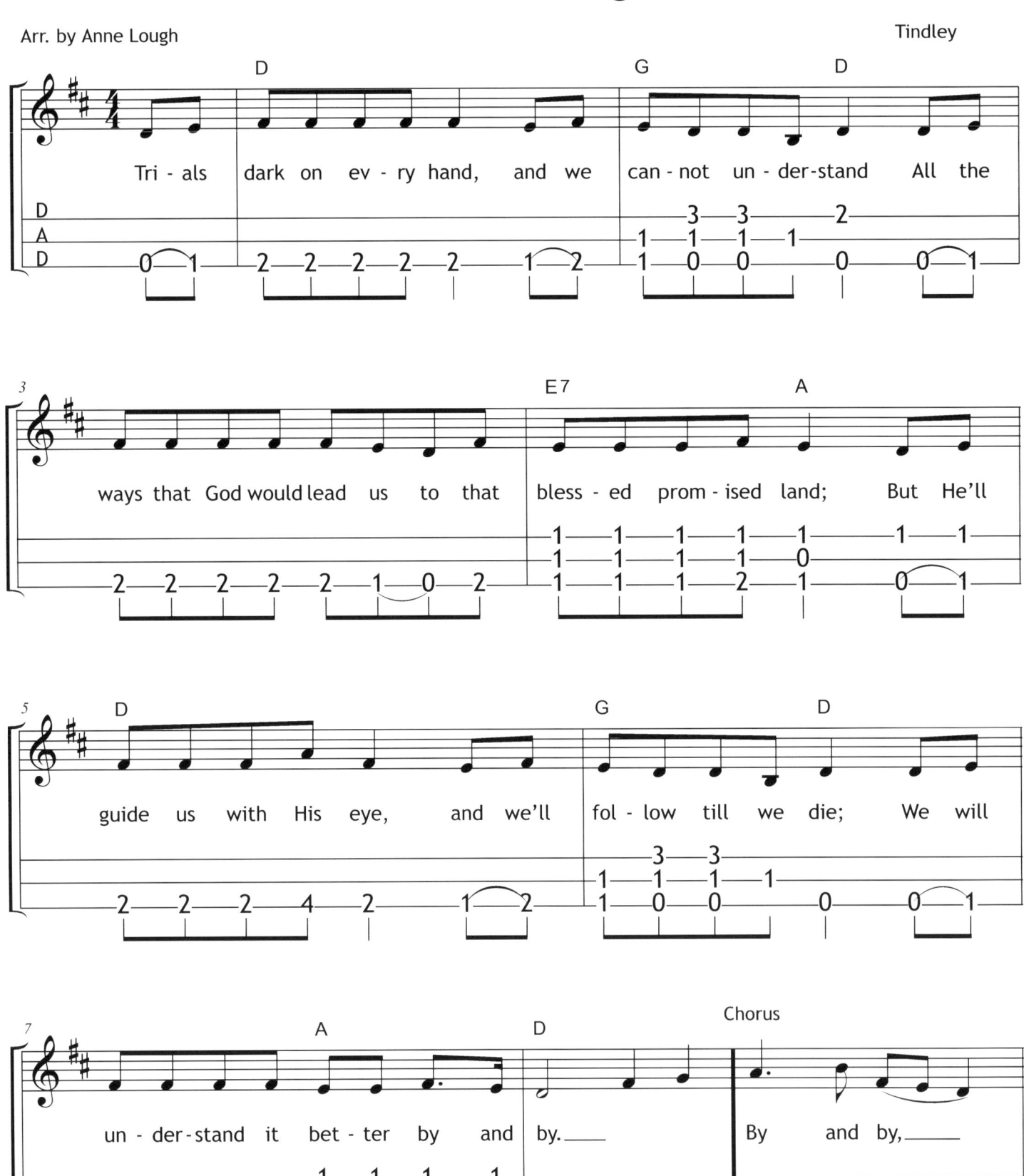

2. Oft our cherished plans have failed, disappointments have prevailed,
And we've wandered in the darkness, heavyhearted and alone;
But we're trusting in the Lord, and, according to His Word,
We will understand it better by and by.
               Chorus

3. Temptations, hidden snares often take us unawares,
And our hearts are made to bleed for some tho'tless word or deed,
And we wonder why the test when we try to do our best,
But we'll understand it better by and by.
               Chorus

When They Ring the Golden Bells

Arr. by Anne Lough

Dion de Marbello

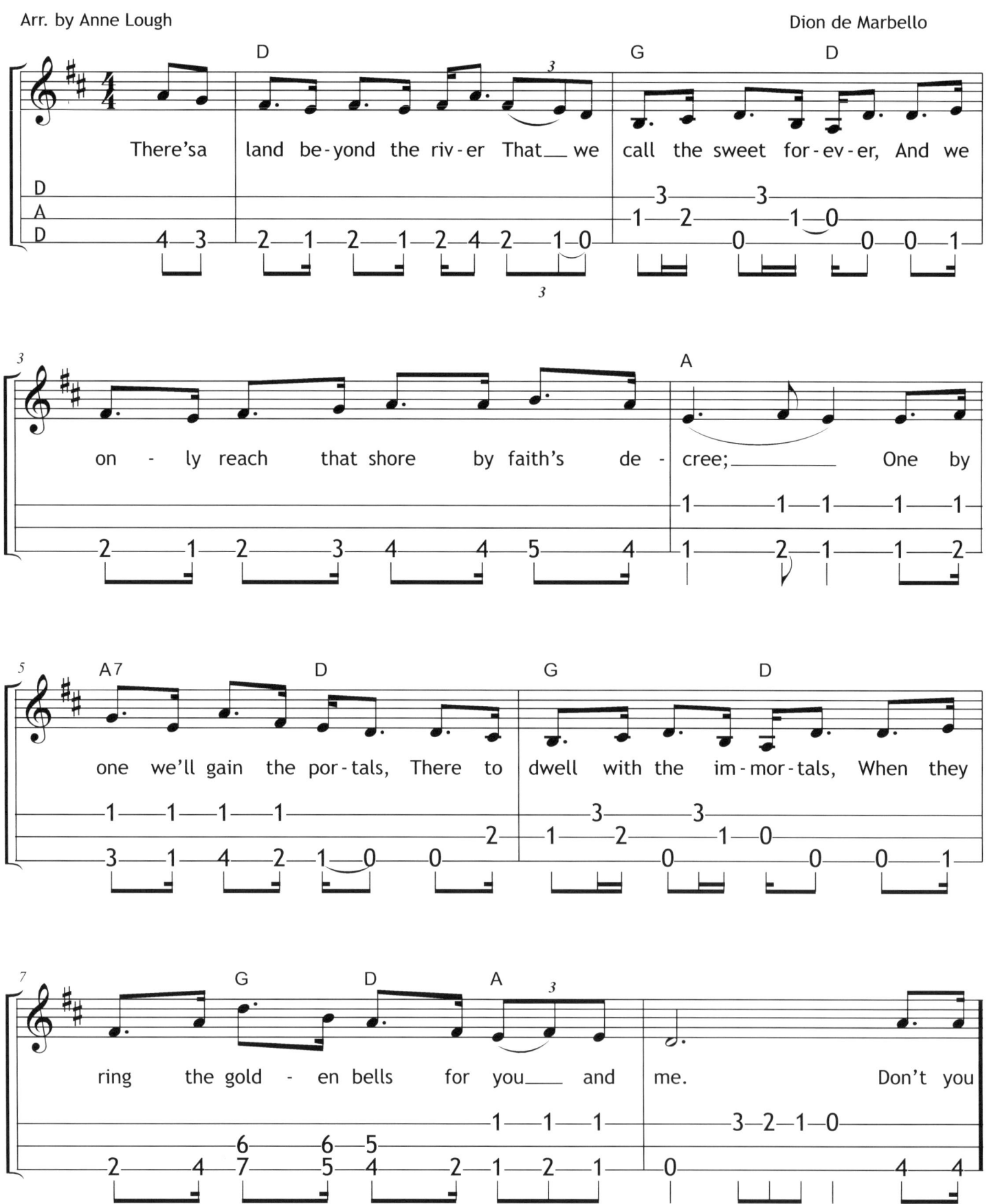

2. When our days shall know their number, When in death we sweetly slumber,
When the King commands the spirit to be free;
Nevermore with anguish laden, We shall reach that lovely Eden,
When they ring the golden bells for you and me.
                Chorus

3. We shall know no sin or sorrow, In that haven of tomorrow,
When our barque shall sail beyond the crystal sea;
We shall only know the blessing Of our Father's sweet caressing,
When they ring the golden bells for you and me.
                Chorus

Where We'll Never Grow Old

Arr. by Anne Lough

Moore

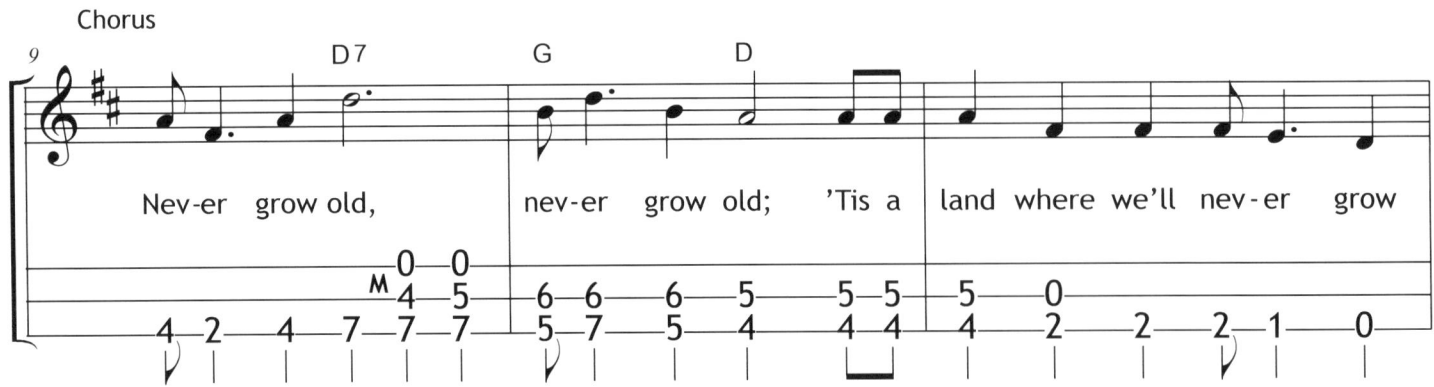

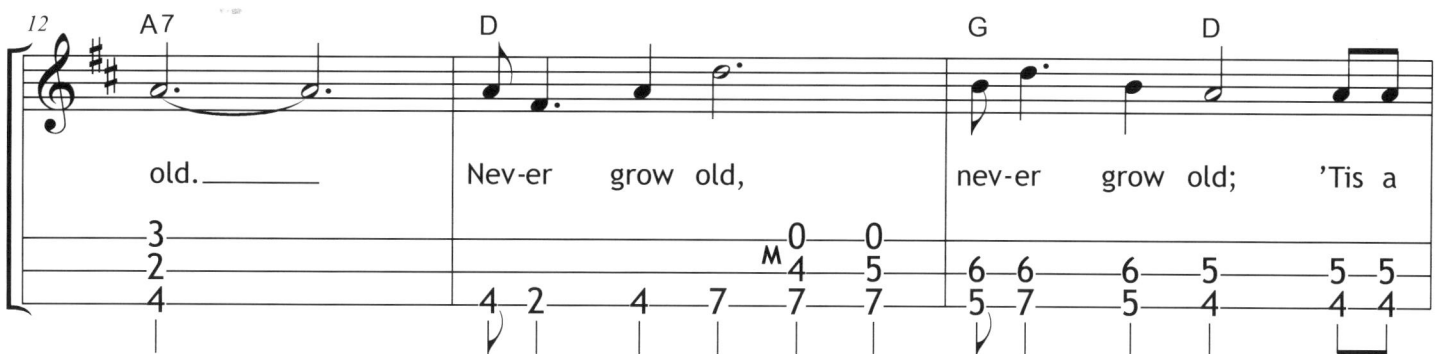

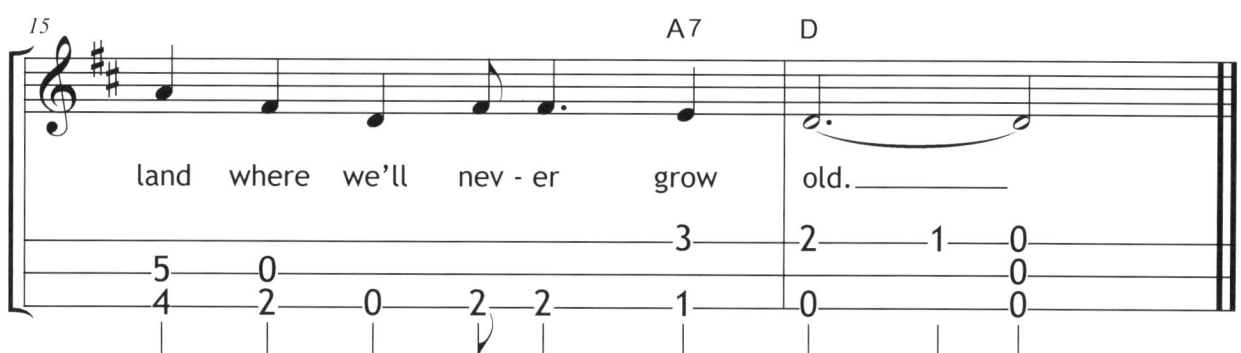

2. In that beautiful home where we'll never more roam,
We shall be in the sweet by and by;
Happy praise to the King, thru eternity sing,
'Tis a land where we never shall die.
                    Chorus

3. When our work here is done and the life crown is won,
And our troubles and trials are o'er;
All our sorrow will end, and our voices will blend,
With the loved ones who've gone on before.
                    Chorus

Whispering Hope

Arr. by Anne Lough

Hawthorne

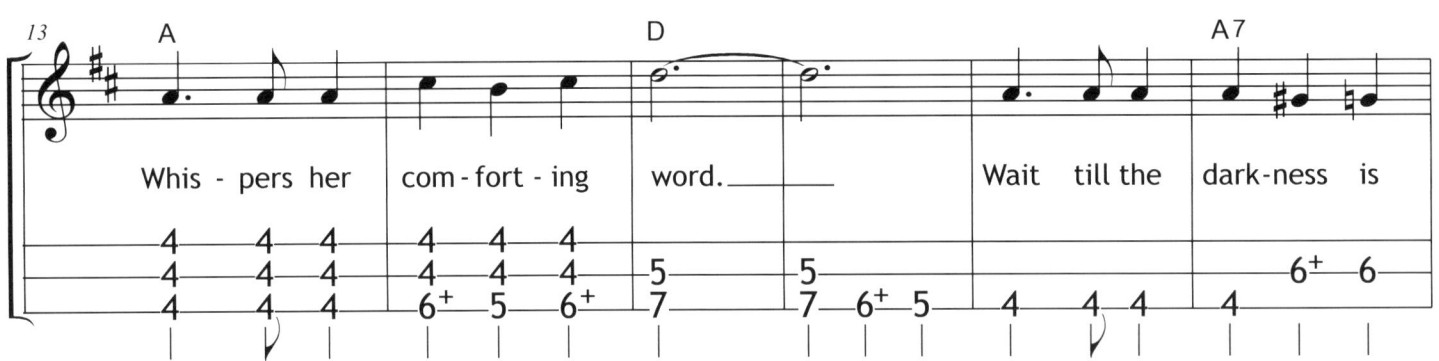
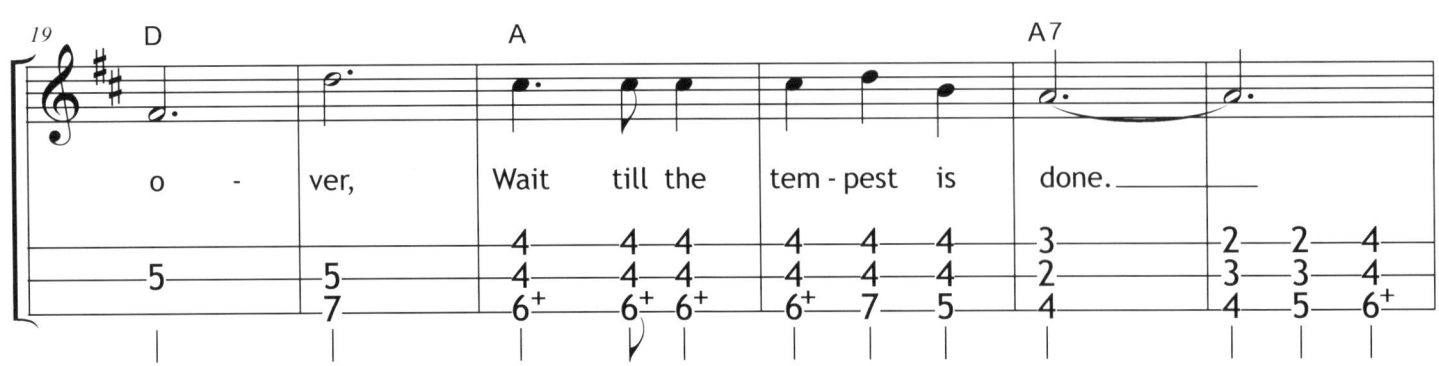

2. If, in the darkness of twilight, Dim be the region afar,
Will not the deepening darkness Brighten the glimmering star?
Then, when the night is upon us, Why should the heart sink away?
When the dark midnight is over, Watch for the breaking of day.
                Chorus

3. Hope, as an anchor so steadfast, Rends the dark veil for the soul,
Whither the Master has entered, Robbing the grave of its goal.
Come, then, O come glad fruition, Come to my sad, weary heart,
Come, O thou blest hope of glory, Never, O never depart.
                Chorus

Reverse Ionian or DGD

Who says dulcimers always have to play in the key of D? Here is a quick and easy way to re-tune to the **key of G** from the DAD tuning.

Keep the bass and melody strings tuned to **D**. Re-tune the middle string from A down one step to G. This pitch can be sounded by plucking the bass string while holding down the 3rd fret.

You are now tuned in **Reverse Ionian (DGD)**. The 3rd fret on the melody string is now the starting point, or **Do**, of the scale, as it was in the Ionian tuning, but now you are playing in the key of **G**. The scale would be played just as in Ionian, starting on the 3rd fret and playing up to the 10th fret, using the 6th fret instead of the 61/2. The **G**, or I chord would again be outlined by playing the 3rd, 5th, 7th and 10th frets.

The **Do-Sol**, or **1-5** relationship is still maintained (for the key of G) but the **Do** is now on the middle string and the sol on the bass and melody strings. Hence, the term **Reverse Ionian**.

The remaining six songs of the book are in this tuning. Because of their melodic range, these tunes are more "singable" in the key of G for most voices. Changing to this tuning also gives a brightness to the songs that would not be heard in DAD.

Another quick way to play in G is to use a capo on the 3rd fret in the DAD tuning. I chose to use DGD instead for these tunes because of their melodic range. More of the melody notes can be played on the melody string, giving a fuller, more old time sound to these cherished hymns.

Dwelling in Beulah Land

Arr. by Anne Lough

Miles

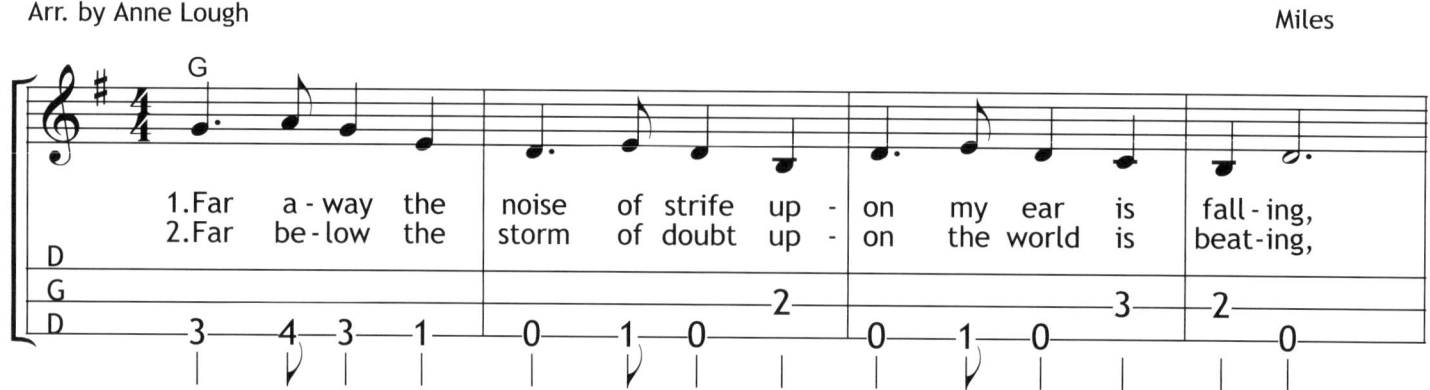
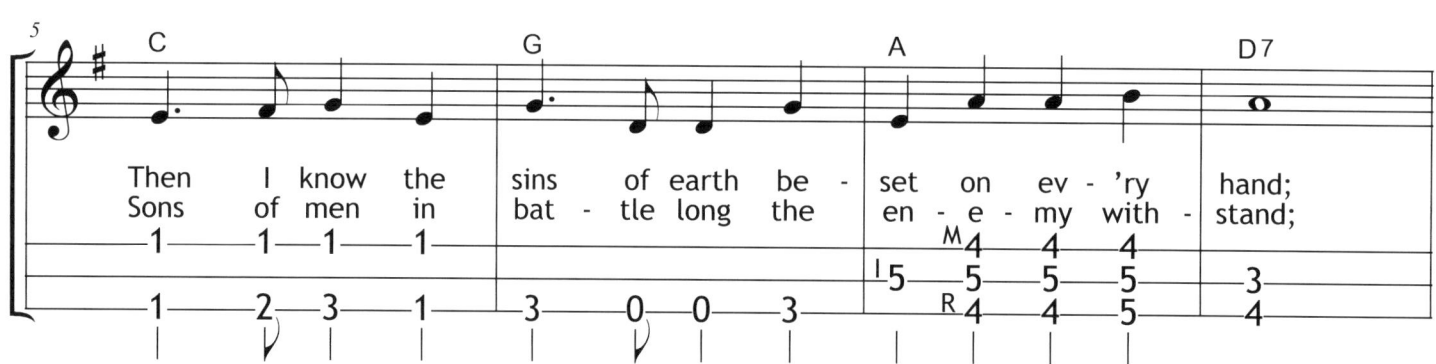
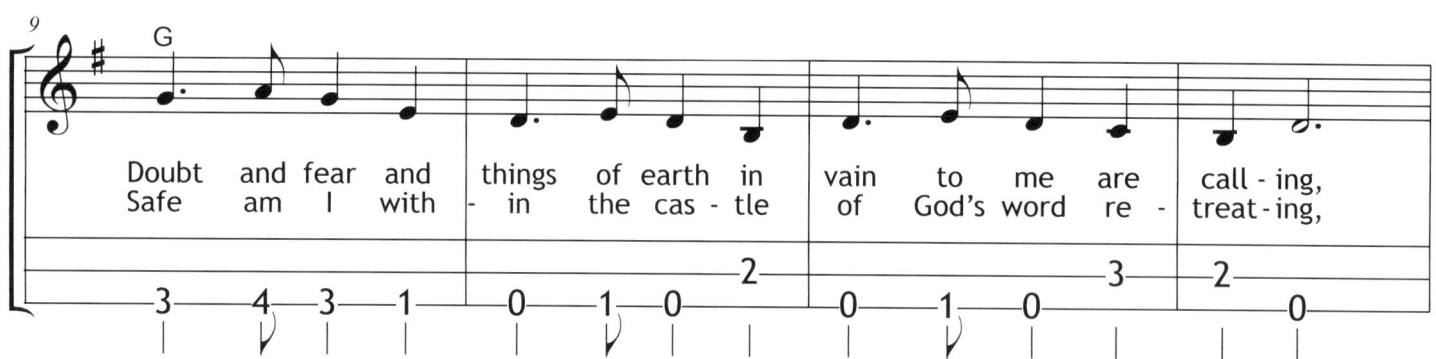
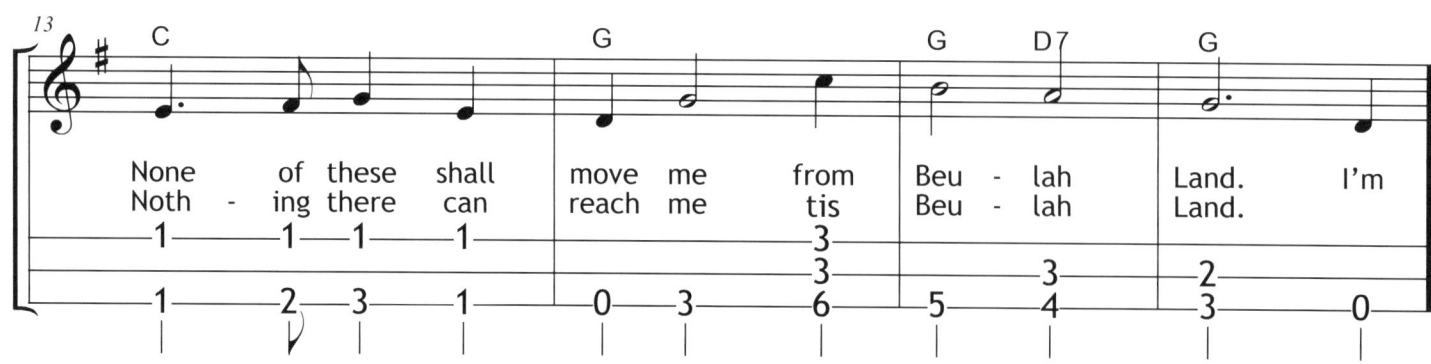

3. Let the stormy breezes blow, their cry cannot alarm me,
I am safely sheltered here, protected by God's hand;
Here the sun is always shining, here there's naught can harm me,
I am safe forever in Beulah Land.
      Chorus

4. Viewing here the works of God, I sink in contemplation,
Hearing now His blessed voice, I see the way He planned;
Dwelling in the Spirit, here I learn of full salvation,
Gladly will I tarry in Beulah Land.
      Chorus

For the Beauty of the Earth

Arr. by Anne Lough

Pierpoint/Kocher

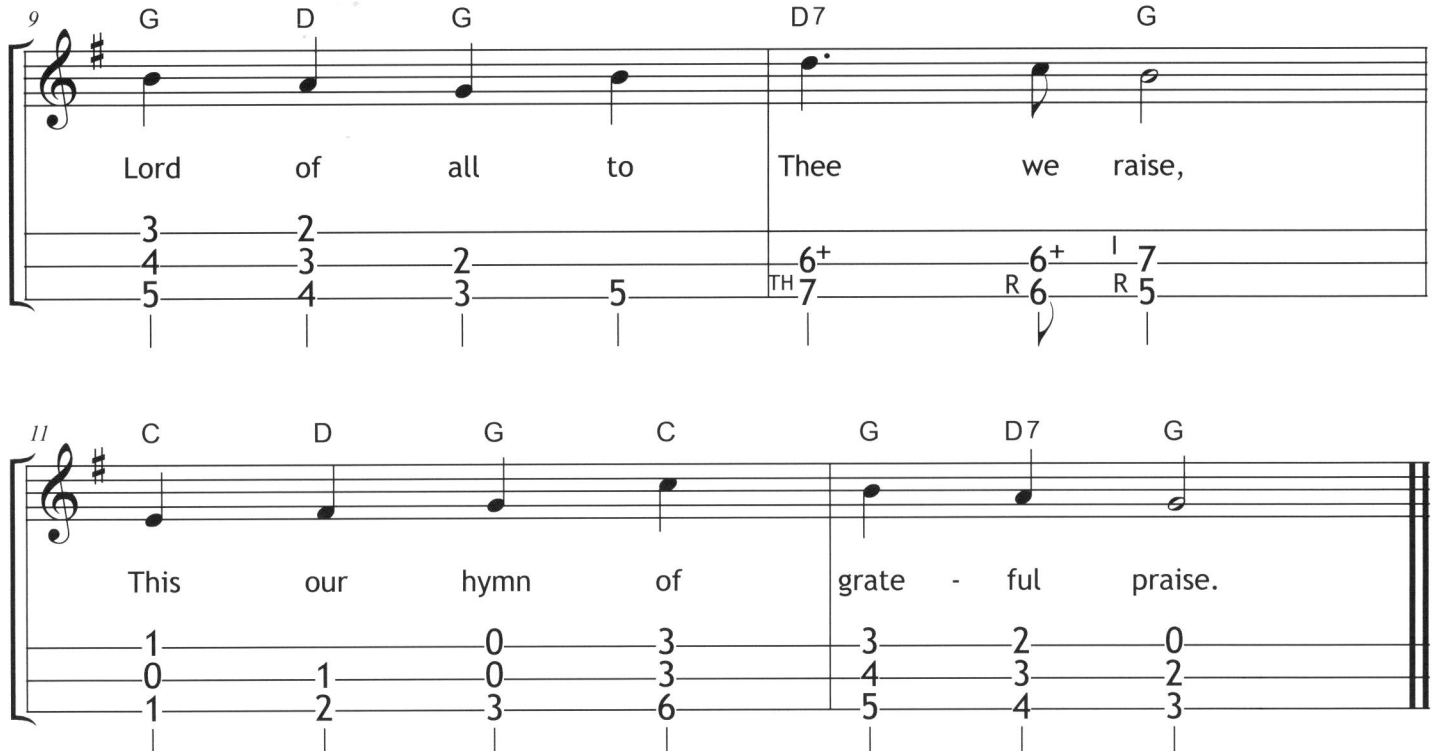

2. For the wonder of each hour, Of the day and of the night,
Hill and vale and tree and flow'r, Sun and moon and stars of light;
Lord of all to Thee we raise This our hymn of grateful praise.

3. For the joy of human love, Brother, sister, parent, child.
Friends on earth and friends above, For all gentle thoughts and mild;
Lord of all to Thee we raise This our hymn of grateful praise.

4. For the church that evermore Lifteth holy hands above,
Off'ring up on ev'ry shore Her pure sacrifice of love;
Lord of all to Thee we raise This our hymn of grateful praise.

5. For the joy of ear and eye, For the heart and mind's delight,
For the mystic harmony Linking sense to sound and sight;
Lord of all to Thee we raise This our hymn of grateful praise.

6. For Thyself, best Gift Divine! To our race so freely giv'n,
For that great, great love of Thine, Peace on earth, and joy in heav'n;
Lord of all to Thee we raise This our hymn of grateful praise.

I Love to Tell the Story

Arr. by Anne Lough

Hankey/Fischer

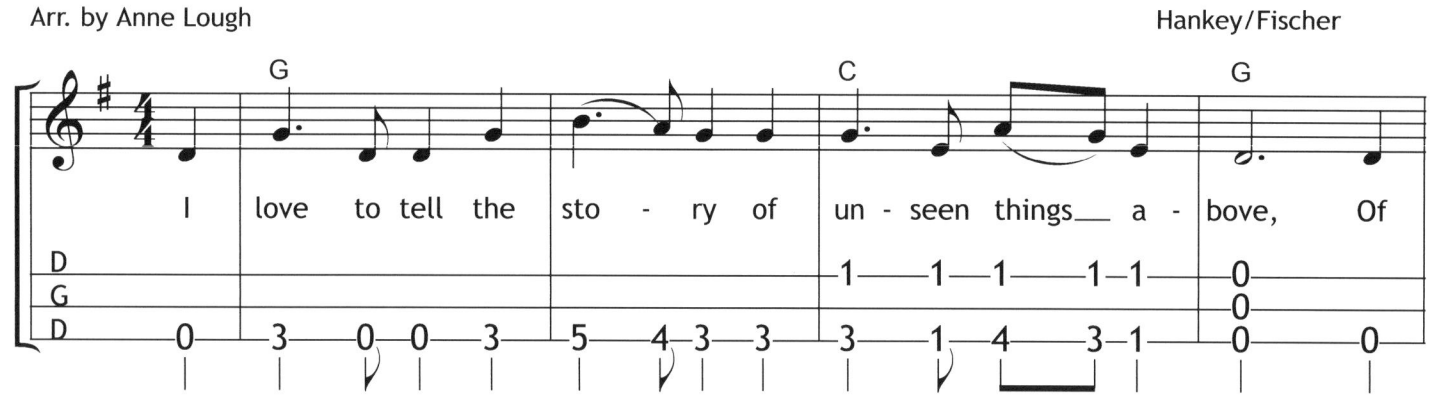
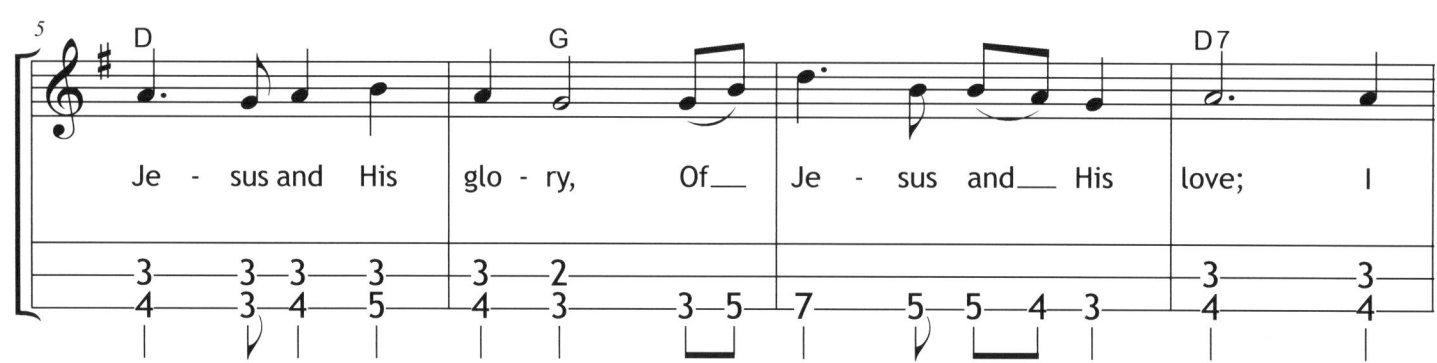
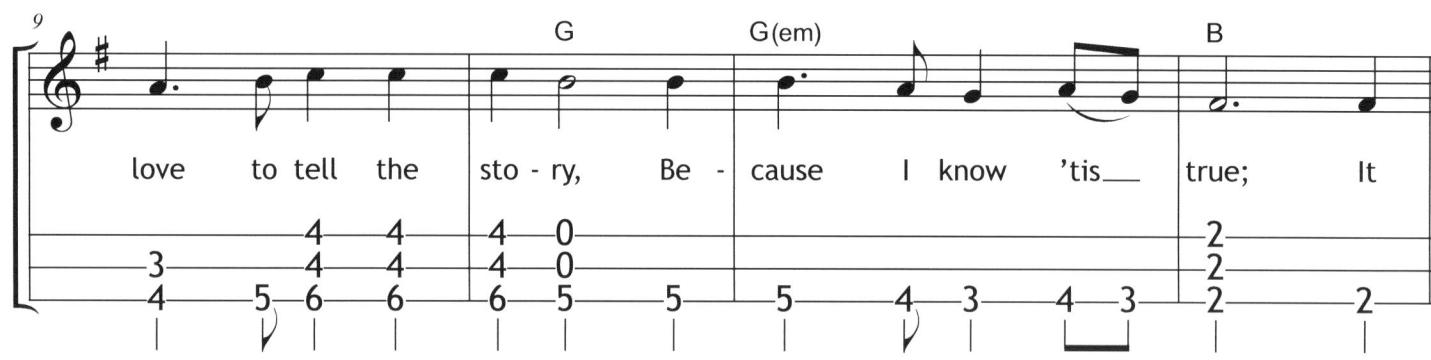
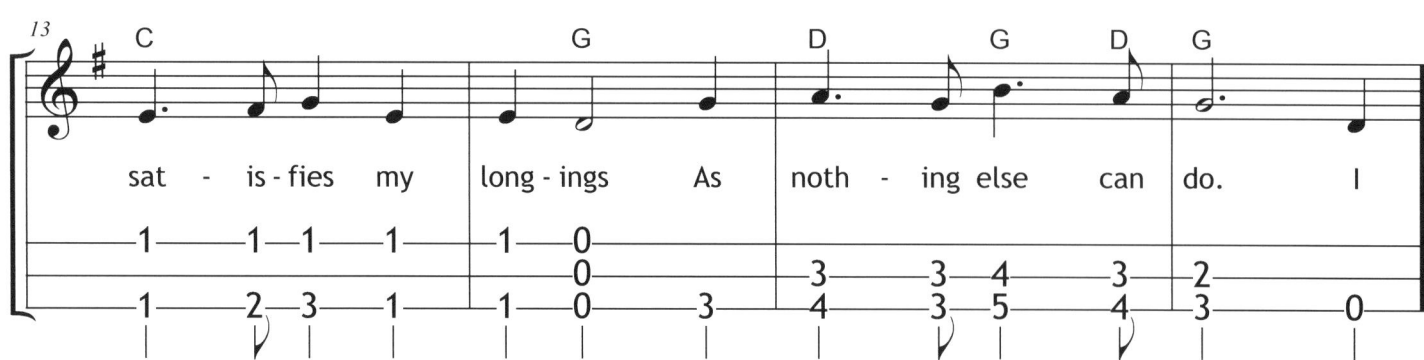

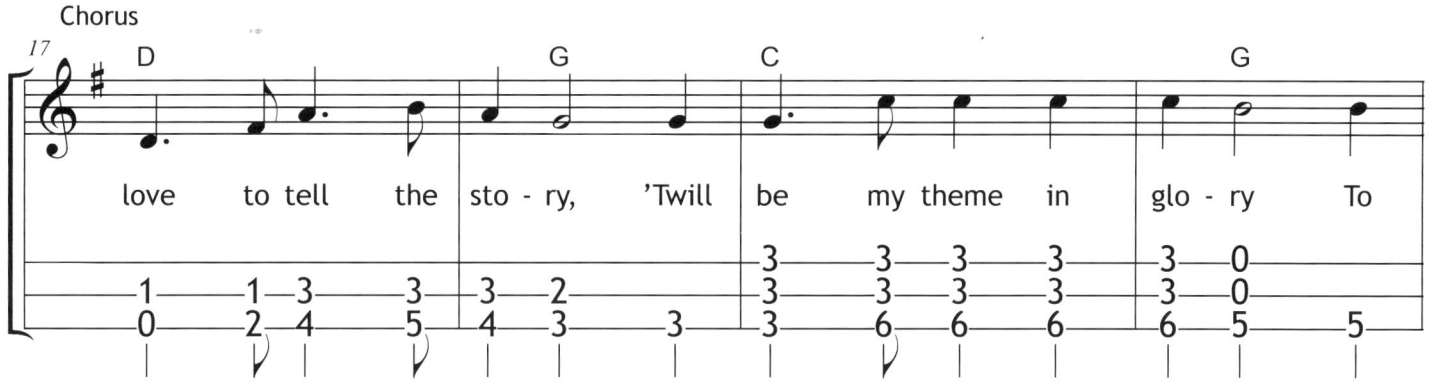
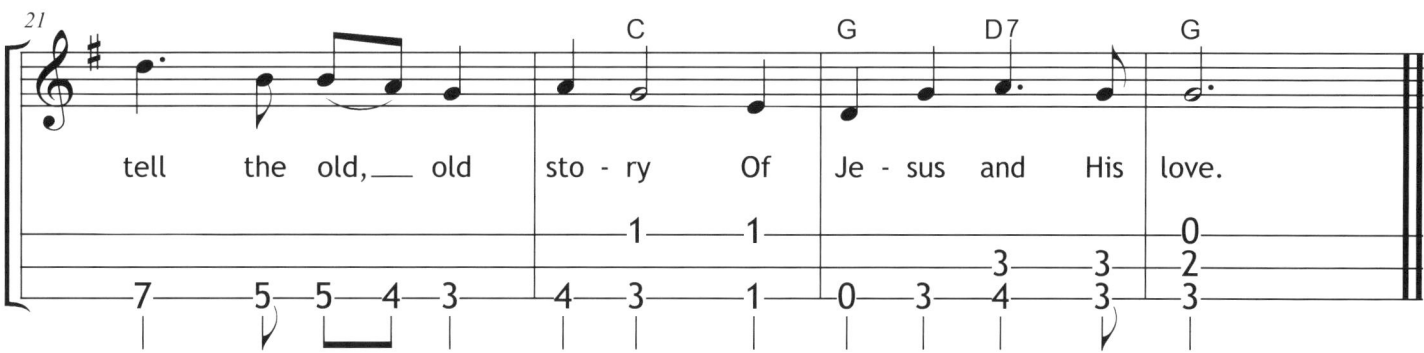

2. I love to tell the story, 'Tis pleasant to repeat
What seems each time I tell it, More wonderfully sweet;
I love to tell the story, For some have never heard
The message of salvation From God's own holy Word.
      Chorus

3. I love to tell the story; For those who know it best
Seem hungering and thirsting To hear it, like the rest;
And when, in scenes of glory, I sing the new, new song,
'Twill be the old, old story That I have loved so long.
      Chorus

In the Garden

Arr. by Anne Lough
Miles

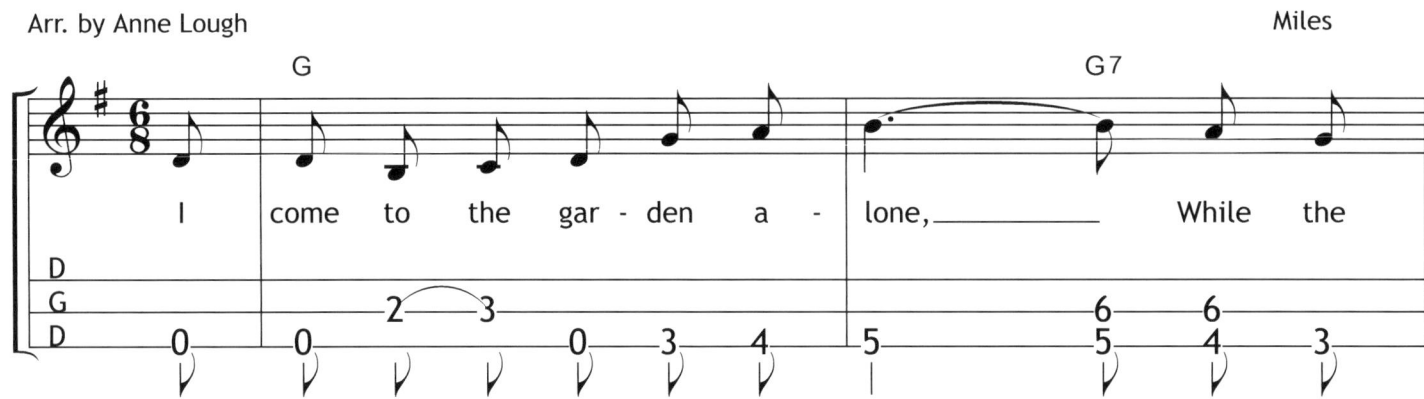
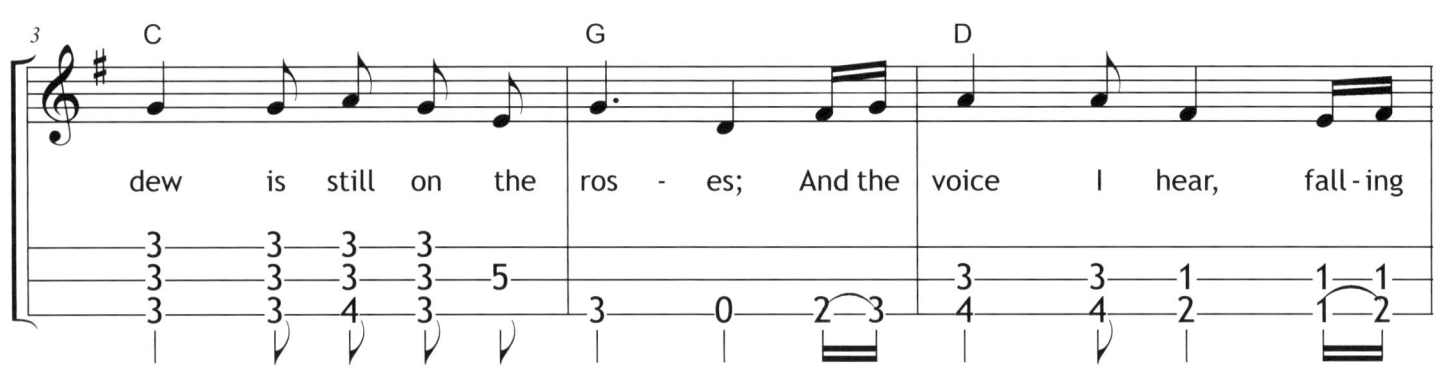
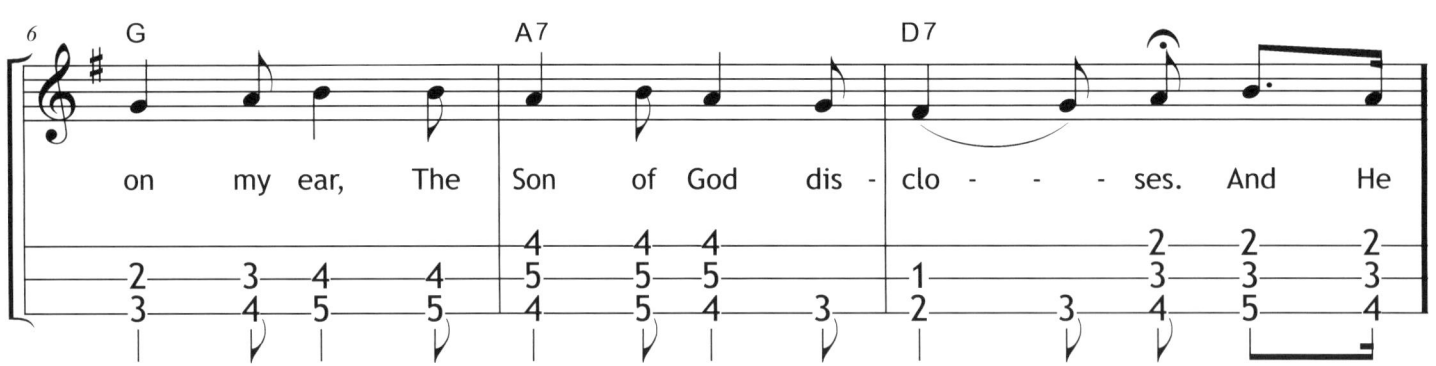
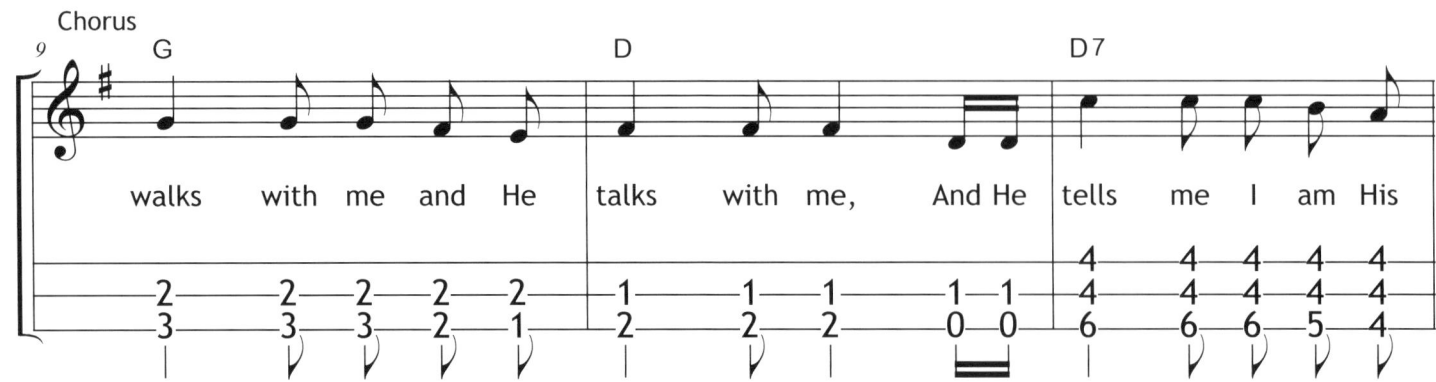

2. He speaks and the sound of His voice
Is so sweet the birds hush their singing;
And the melody that He gave to me,
Within my heart is ringing.
     Chorus

3. I'd stay in the garden with Him,
Tho' the night around me be falling;
But He bids me go, thro' the voice of woe,
His voice to me is calling.
     Chorus

Rock of Ages

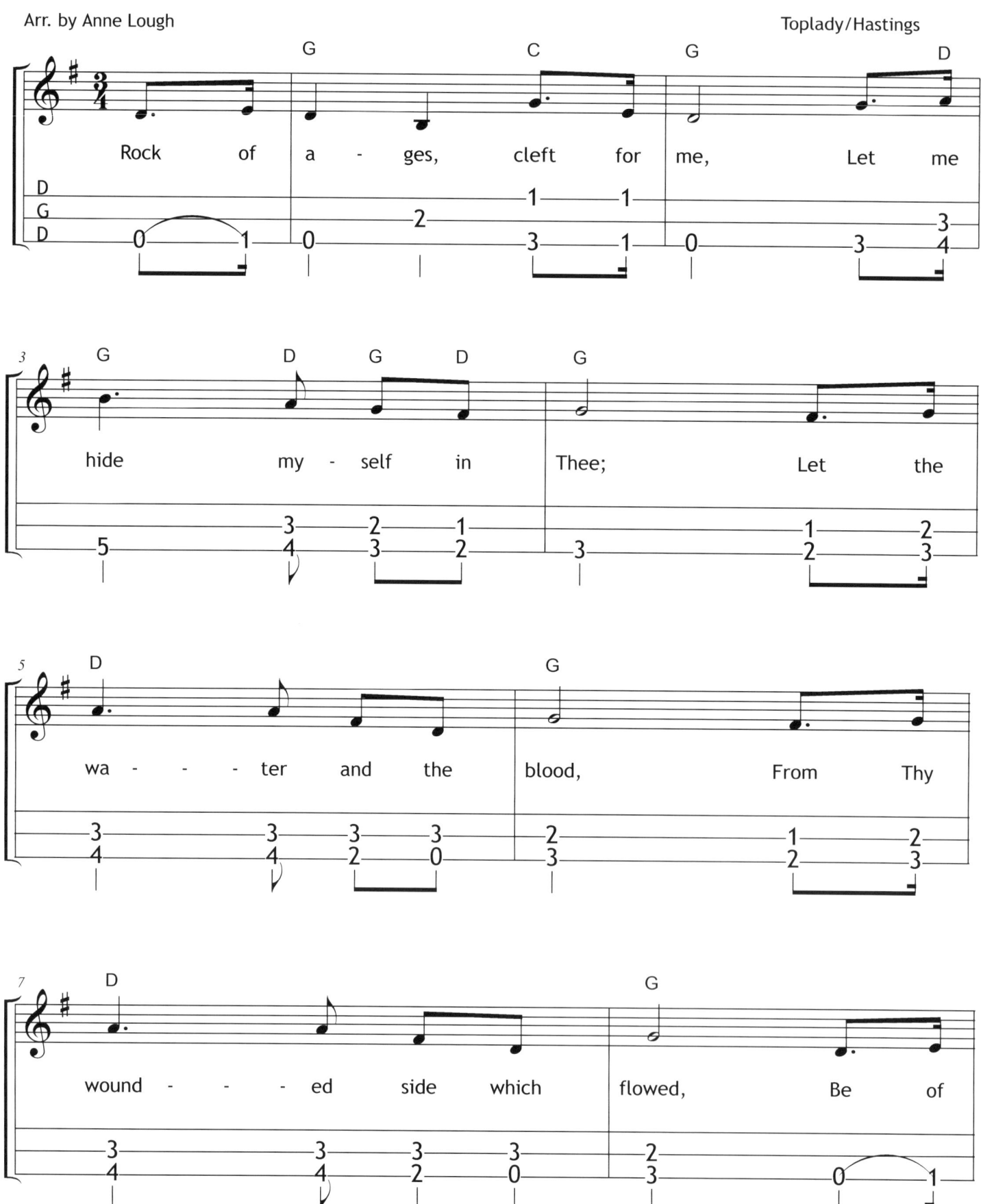

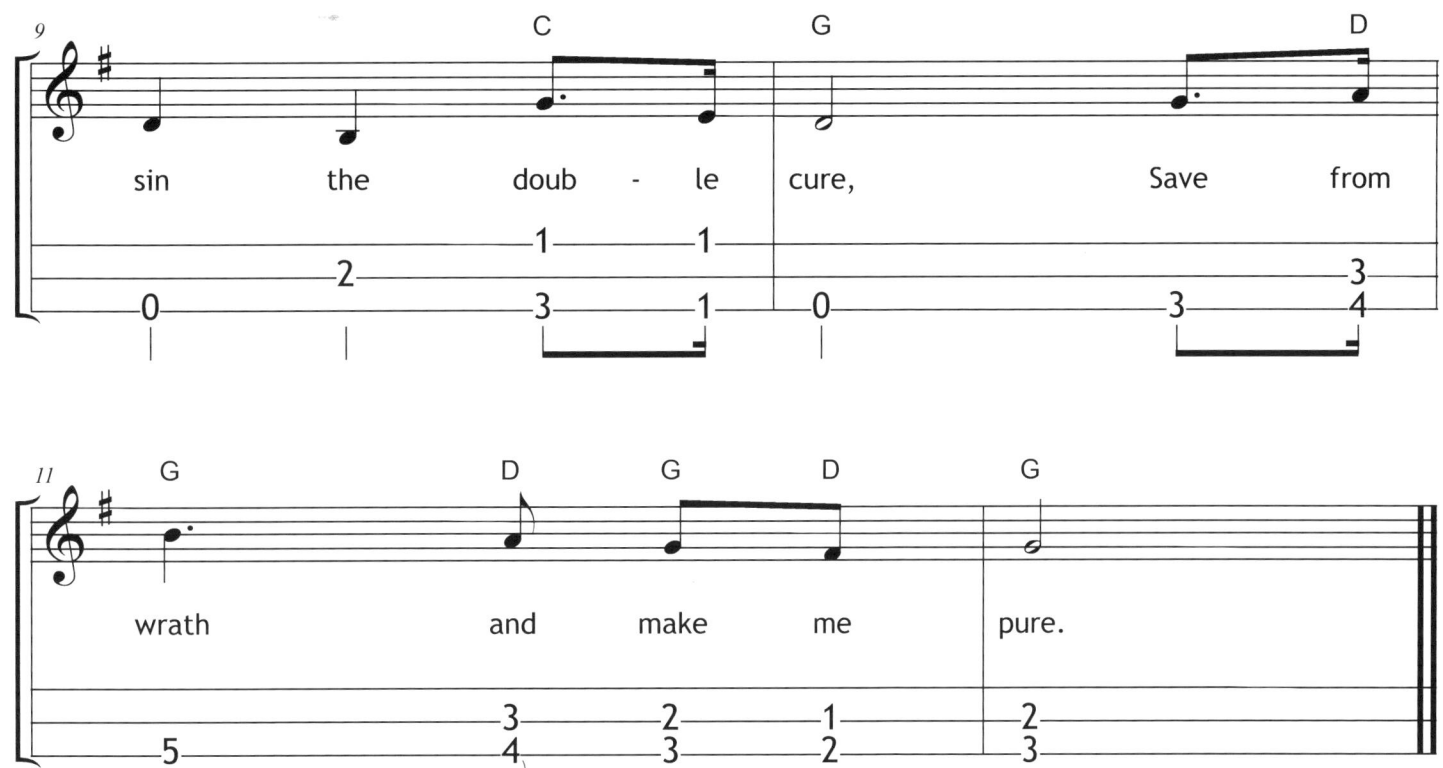

2. Not the labors of my hands Can fulfill Thy law's demands;
These for sin could not atone; Thou must save, and Thou alone;
In my hand no price I bring, Simply to Thy cross I cling.

3. While I draw this fleeting breath, When mine eyes shall close in death,
When I rise to worlds unknown, And behold Thee on Thy throne,
Rock of ages, cleft for me, Let me hide myself in Thee.

Victory in Jesus

Arr. by Anne Lough

Bartlett

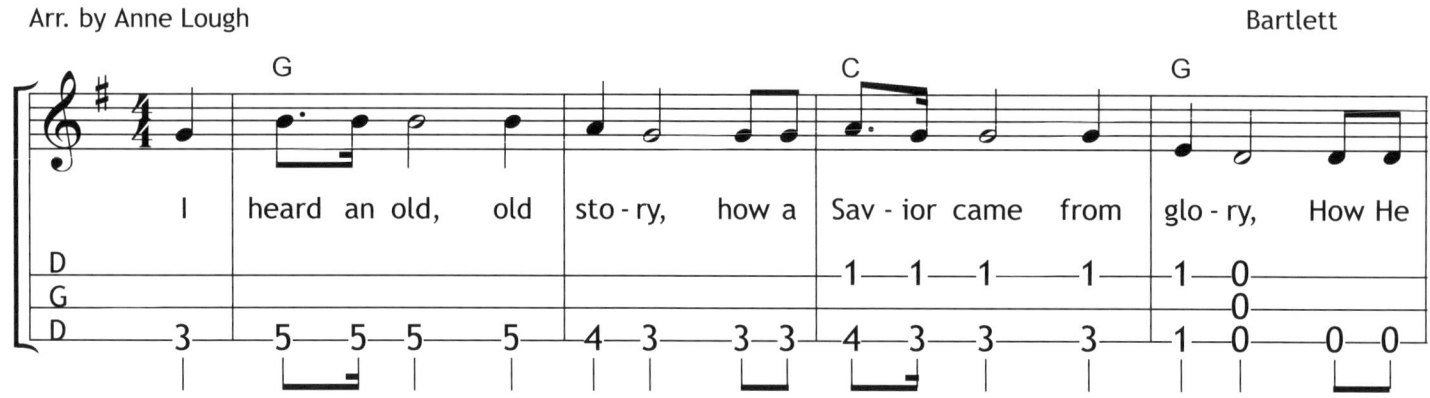
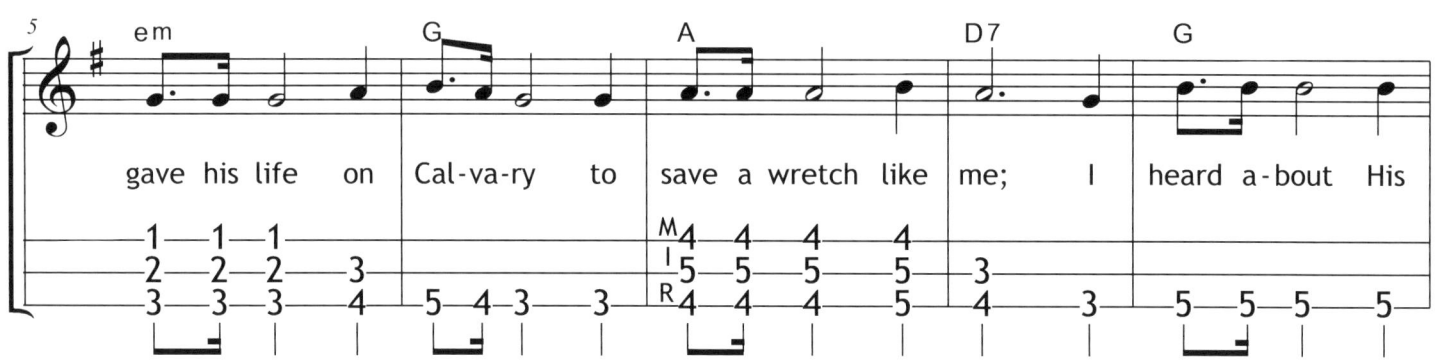
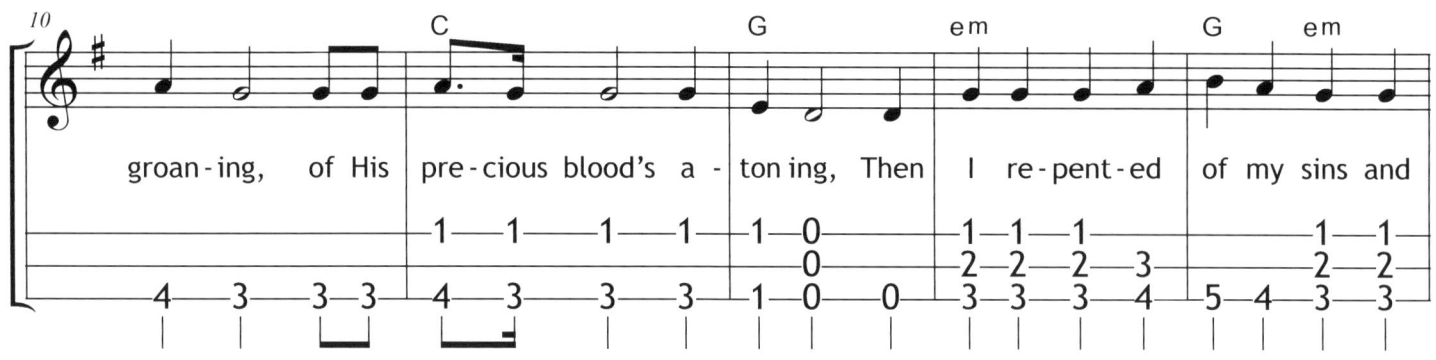
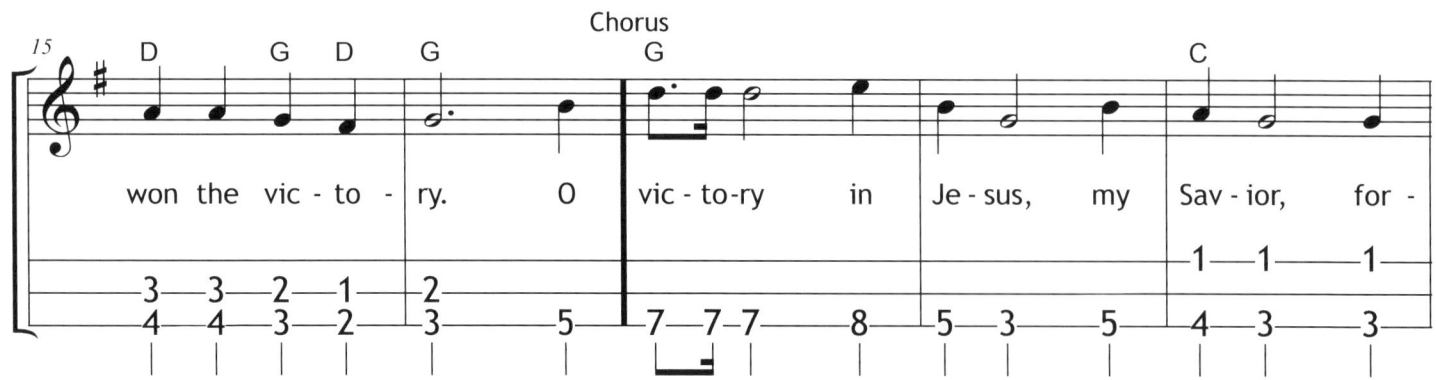

2. I heard about his healing, of His cleansing pow'r revealing,
How He made the lame to walk again and caused the blind to see;
And then I cried, "Dear Jesus, come and heal my broken spirit,"
And somehow Jesus came and bro't to me the victory.
		Chorus

3. I heard about a mansion He has built for me in glory,
And I heard about the streets of gold beyond the crystal sea;
About the angels singing, and the old redemption story,
And some sweet day I'll sing up there the song of victory.
		Chorus

About the Author

A native of Springfield, Virginia, Anne Lough began playing and singing folk music at the age of fourteen. She has continued to share her love of music through the years while raising four daughters and completing a Music Education Degree from Murray State University, Murray, Ky., and a Master of Music Education Degree from Western Carolina University, Cullowhee, NC. Anne now resides in the mountains of North Carolina and devotes her time to festivals, workshops, performances, Exploritas classes and school residencies. Equally at home on the guitar, autoharp, mountain and hammered dulcimer, her educational programs and performances range from traditional music and folk songs to shaped note singing, classical and American popular music, folk dance traditions, storytelling, folklore and cultural history.

In addition to being a frequent instructor in mountain and hammered dulcimer at the prestigious John C. Campbell Folk School in Brasstown, NC, Anne has taught at the Swannanoa Gathering, Western Carolina Dulcimer Week, Augusta Heritage Dulcimer Week, Buckeye Dulcimer Festival and at numerous other festivals and workshops throughout the country. Her artistic interpretation, sensitive playing style, versatility, creative arranging and skill as an instructor have earned her national acclaim. Anne has been on the Touring Artist Roster for the North Carolina Arts Council for many years and is active in schools in many states as a Visiting Artist.

Anne's music can be heard on a number of recordings, Smoky Mountain educational videos, public radio and a recent North Carolina PBS Christmas Special. She has also published several collections of arrangements for the mountain and hammered dulcimer.

Photo by Chris Bartol. Used by Permission.